Are You Dying for a Drink?

TEENAGERS AND ALCOHOL ABUSE

Laurel Graeber

Julian Messner  New York

JULIAN MESSNER and colophon are
trademarks of Simon & Schuster, Inc.

Manufactured in the United States of America
Library of Congress Cataloging in Publication Data

Graeber, Laurel.
    Are you dying for a drink?

    (Teen survival library)
    Includes index.
    Summary: Discusses what it is like to be a teen-ager who drinks too much,
who is likely to become an alcoholic, why teens drink, alcohol's effect on body
and mind, drinking and driving, and living with alcoholic parents.

HV5135.G73 1985   362.2'92'088055   85-8880

ISBN: 0-671-50818-0 (MCE)
ISBN: 0-671-63112-8 (pbk.)

10 9 8 7 6 5 4 3 2 (MCE)
10 9 8 7 6 5 4 3 2 1 (pbk.)

All names in this book are pseudonyms, except those of clinical professionals and those of individuals who agreed to be identified in full by first and last names.

I would like to thank the following individuals for their advice and assistance in the preparation of this book: Robert Anastas, Executive Director, SADD . . . Dr. Sheila Blume, Medical Director of Alcoholism and Compulsive Gambling Programs, South Oaks Hospital, Amityville, N.Y. . . . Carla Boden, Associate Producer, "That Teen Show" . . . Jon Bruno, Public Relations Director, Daytop Village, Inc. . . . Dr. Ross Brower, Assistant Professor of Public Health and Psychiatry and Assistant Attending Physician, New York Hospital-Cornell Medical Center . . . Irene R. Bush, Director, Children of Alcoholics Foundation . . . Charles Butler, Manager, Driver Education Programs, Automobile Association of America . . . Beth Curley, Executive producer, "SOAPBOX" . . . Dr. Geoffrey M. Graeber, Director, Division of Surgery, Walter Reed Army Institute of Research . . . Ellen Morehouse, Director, Student Assistance Program . . . John W. Palmer, Coordinator, The Control Factor . . . Diane Purcell, Assistant Manager, Youth Unit, Parkside Lodge . . . Ms. Brenda Stanislawski, Executive Director, The Ozaukee Council on Alcohol and Other Drug Abuse . . . Mr. Robert Steele, Coordinator, Ohio Teen Institute . . . Margaret Thayer, Alcohol, Other Drugs and Highway Safety consultant, Maine Division of Alcohol and Drug Education Services . . . Robert Ulrich, Executive Director, National Student Safety Program . . . Dr. William C. Van Ost and Elaine Van Ost, The Van Ost Institute for Family Living . . . Madeline Whitlock, Secretary, A.A. World Services, Inc. . . . *Young Miss Magazine.* . . . Joanne Yurman, Director of Prevention and Education, National Council on Alcoholism . . . and finally, all those young adults who so graciously gave of their time and energy to be interviewed for this project.

For my family
and especially my husband,
Michael Buxbaum . . .

Table of Contents

CHAPTER ONE
Drinking: What's the Problem? / **11**

CHAPTER TWO
Who Becomes an Alcoholic? / **27**

CHAPTER THREE
Bottled Trouble: Why Teenagers Drink / **39**

CHAPTER FOUR
Alcohol and Your Body and Mind / **51**

CHAPTER FIVE
Hell on Wheels: Drinking and Driving / **75**

CHAPTER SIX
Family Secret, Family Disease / **99**

CHAPTER SEVEN
Where To Go for Help / **121**

Appendix / **145**

Bibliography / **151**

Index / **155**

CHAPTER ONE

Drinking:
What's the Problem?

IT'S 7:15 ON A WEEKDAY morning, and Sandy, thirteen, has just awakened. Her mother has already left for work, and Sandy knows she has the house to herself. Going to the liquor cabinet, she takes out a bottle of Puerto Rican rum—her favorite drink—and pours a shot. She downs it quickly and then looks at the other bottles. Removing the Canadian whiskey, she decides not to bother with her empty glass. She removes the cap and takes a long gulp. She's now ready to get dressed for school, but not before she puts some beer aside to take with her. Sandy doesn't like to be without liquor during the day—in its absence, she feels nervous and has the shakes.

In school, Sandy finds it hard to concentrate. In sixth grade, she was in a special program for gifted students, but since she started drinking daily about a year ago, her grades have plunged and she's been put back in average classes. She's also quit the yearbook and the gymnastics team because she would prefer to spend her time and money on alcohol. The only school activity she still looks forward to is chorus, because her friends have "rush" (amyl nitrate) there, one of the many substances Sandy likes to combine with alcohol. They manage to sneak the drug during practice.

By the middle of the day, Sandy is ready for another drink. She's hidden a beer in her purse, where she can easily take it unnoticed to the girls' room. She drinks there, and later in the afternoon decides to cut school in order to have more. She drinks about another quarter of a small bottle of Puerto Rican rum. By now, going back to school is too dangerous—one time when she returned to class drunk, her teacher sent her to the guidance counselor, who called her mother. Sandy's mother, who's divorced, has tried punishing her to stop her behavior, but Sandy always manages to sneak drinks.

After Sandy gets home, she has more whiskey. Eventually, she falls into a drunken sleep. But this might not signal the end of her day—sometimes she even gets up in the middle of the night to have a drink in the hallway outside her room.

Peter, fourteen, has a lot in common with Sandy. Although he once drank only on the weekends, he now drinks much more frequently—about every other day. On the average, he has two six-packs of beer and "a couple of shots of whatever." He frequently mixes alcohol with other drugs, including marijuana and mescaline. Once an average to good

12

student, Peter seldom goes to school anymore. Instead, he has a keg party at home.

As soon as Peter gets up, he looks forward to drinking. Although his favorite drink is beer, he sometimes starts out with hard liquor. He's been known to drink quantities that, in his words, "would kill an elephant." Once, he and a friend drank an entire bottle of whiskey, followed by some beer. His friend became delirious, and was crying and screaming. Peter, terrified, was relieved when his friend finally calmed down and went to sleep. But when he woke up, he was still drunk. Peter became frightened, and although intoxicated himself, he carried his friend home.

Today, Peter has managed to get to school. But he's very drunk—so drunk that he can barely sit up. In his third period class, in front of the teacher and the other students, he falls out of his chair. School officials call his family. This time, Peter is the one carried home.

Sandy and Peter are real people, although these are not their real names. The vignettes you have just read concern events that took place a few years ago. Sandy is now sixteen and Peter is eighteen. Both have obtained treatment for their alcohol and chemical abuse from Daytop Village, a program with facilities throughout New York State. Neither one now drinks. But could Sandy and Peter have been considered teenage alcoholics?

First, let's take a look at what alcoholism is. The National Council on Alcoholism (NCA), a New York City–based organization devoted to alcohol education and the prevention of alcohol abuse, defines alcoholism as a disease. This doesn't mean, of course, that alcoholism is an illness in the sense that chicken pox or mumps are. Instead, the term *disease* has been used as a model for understanding the way alcoholism affects the body and mind.

Alcoholism is considered a disease because its victims have no control over its progress. Once someone has become addicted to the drug alcohol (and alcohol *is* a drug), he or she no longer has the power to stop drinking. Like other addicts, alcoholics are psychologically dependent on the drug. Even more important, they are physically dependent. Alcoholics who are deprived of alcohol experience symptoms of physical withdrawal that include anxiety, violent tremors, and nightmarish hallucinations. Some of the bodily effects of withdrawal are life-threatening. In fact, before modern medicine invented ways to treat alcohol withdrawal, a full 35 percent of people suffering from *delirium tremens* (the medical term for withdrawal) died of it. And despite medical advances, alcoholics still have two to four times the mortality rate of the rest of the population. This is because alcoholism results in damage to almost all parts of the body, particularly the liver, brain, nervous system, and digestive system. If alcoholism is unarrested, these changes become irreversible and finally fatal.

In addition to being potentially fatal, alcoholism is defined as *chronic* and *progressive*. In other words, the physical and emotional changes accumulate over time and increase in severity. Sandy, for example, noticed that she had the shakes if she didn't drink every day. If she had continued to drink at the same rate until she was thirty-five, she might have experienced worse symptoms. She might have been diagnosed as having liver disease. That's assuming, of course, that she lived that long. Sandy had already had one brush with death at age twelve. She was so drunk that she started to cross a street without looking for cars. She was prevented from being hit only because a friend pulled her out of the way.

Just knowing what alcoholism is, however, doesn't make it easy for even skilled clinicians to make a diagnosis. Today, some physicians prefer not to use the term *alcoholic,* but refer to a patient as *alcohol-dependent.* One of the reasons is that alcoholism is not a yesterday-you-didn't-have-it-today-you-do phenomenon. It generally takes years of drinking, usually at the level of five or more drinks a day, to develop the kind of organ damage that indicates the disease. People who drink less than these amounts, however, can still be in danger. People metabolize alcohol differently, and some can suffer negative consequences in their lives at much lower levels. In fact, the harmful effects of drinking on the drinker's ability to function are the most important indicators of alcoholism. The more negative consequences, the more likely it is that the person is an alcoholic.

15

What kind of consequences? Alcoholics usually fail to meet their responsibilities with any consistency. While they may attend school or hold down jobs, they will probably have difficulties in fulfilling their duties. They may call in sick or have to go home early because of drinking. They encounter problems socially, creating embarrassment for themselves or others by behaving inappropriately when drunk. They also tend to drink at socially unacceptable times, such as early in the morning. They may get into trouble with the law, through either drunk driving or some other dangerous or disruptive action. Their family life is also disturbed, because alcoholics cannot meet the needs of spouses, parents, siblings, and children. Their lives center around alcohol.

Alcoholics also experience changes others can't readily observe. They frequently can't remember what happened during an episode of drinking, even though they were fully conscious at the time. (This loss of memory is known as a *blackout.*) They usually have an increased tolerance for alcohol, being able to consume far greater amounts than nonalcoholics and still remain conscious. And even though alcoholics frequently deny that they drink too much, they may inwardly feel anxious and guilty.

Perhaps the most telling criterion, though, is loss of control over drinking. According to the NCA, an alcoholic cannot predict on any given occasion how much he or she will drink, or for how long.

Knowing this, can we say that Sandy and Peter were alcoholics? Sandy had a wide range and variety of alcohol-related symptoms, including those of physical withdrawal—tremors, or as she said, the shakes. Because most teens have not been drinking long enough to develop physical dependency, only a small percentage of them can be considered alcoholics in the medical definition of the word. Sandy, however, who had her first drink at age seven and had been drinking heavily since she was twelve, showed enough dependence to be considered alcoholic by almost any definition. Peter was lucky enough never to have experienced physical withdrawal. Psychologically, though, it was another matter.

"It would just be a rotten day to me—not a full day—when I didn't have a drink," he says.

Even though Peter may not have been an alcoholic in the same sense as an adult who's been drinking for fifteen years, he was certainly a *problem drinker*. This is the term most alcohol professionals use when speaking of teenagers, and it is also defined by the amount a person drinks and the negative consequences he or she experiences. Teenagers like Peter, who get drunk frequently and have resulting difficulties in a number of areas—school, family, friendships, dating, and the law—are problem drinkers.

Both Sandy and Peter, for example, had failing grades as a result of their drinking. Both had problems with their families as well—Sandy's mother finally had to quit her job in order to supervise her daughter. And although neither Sandy nor Peter had been arrested, both had engaged in criminal behav-

17

ior. Sandy had broken into a neighbor's apartment, and Peter had burglarized a house in order to get money for alcohol. He had also driven his father's van without a license.

Most professionals who have studied alcoholism agree that a number of teenagers are like Sandy and Peter. Just how many, however, is a subject of controversy. Some studies have indicated that only 1 to 5 percent of teens are problem drinkers; others have put the figure as high as 31 percent.

Why are these estimates so different? One problem is that many of the studies haven't defined exactly what they mean by *drunk,* and they have only questioned the teenagers in their sample at one point in time. If the study asks questions only about the frequency of drinking and not the amount consumed, a teen may have a few sips of beer several times a week and appear to be a heavy drinker. Others would argue that such a teenager has a behavior problem anyway, because most teenagers are not of legal age to purchase alcohol. Other clinicians have criticized teenage drinking studies for asking adolescents to report their own habits rather than measuring them by more objective means. Heavy drinkers, particularly, may not be reliable about how much they drink. One of the most disturbing indications that teenage drinking may be more of a problem than the statistics show is that most studies have taken place in school. Sandy and Peter and many teens like them wouldn't even have been there to answer the questions. In fact, virtually all the alcohol-abusing teenagers interviewed for this book had cut school frequently or were forced to drop out as a result of their drinking.

Another issue that has made the statistics uncertain is the definition of a problem drinker. Two of the most extensive studies of teenage drinking ever undertaken in the United States were conducted in the 1970s by the Research Triangle Institute (RTI) of Research Triangle Park, North Carolina, under the auspices of the National Institute on Alcohol Abuse and Alcoholism (NIAAA), based in Rockville, Maryland. In their final analysis, the researchers considered the teens surveyed problem drinkers if they had been drunk six or more times in the past year, or if they had experienced alcohol-related problems at least twice in three or more of the following areas: school, friendships, driving, dates, or the police. (In the second survey, family relationships were also included.) The results? Approximately 27 percent were problem drinkers among the 5,428 senior high school students included in the first survey, and 31 percent in the 4,473 senior high students in the second. Other researchers using different criteria would, of course, come up with different figures.

But although some argue that these problem-drinking statistics can't be applied to all U.S. teenagers, the RTI researchers did use their most recent findings to make estimates of drinking patterns among all teens nationally. Approximately 62 percent of teens were estimated to drink at least once a month, and 27 percent to drink at least once a week. Fifteen percent, or more than 1.6 million, were believed to drink heavily (five or more drinks per occasion) once a week or more often.

Interestingly, a less detailed but more recent survey of American teenagers also indicates a high level of alcohol use. The Gallup organization, in Princeton, New Jersey, surveyed a representative nationwide sample of 416 boys and girls, aged thirteen to eighteen, from November 1983 through January 1984. Fifty-nine percent had used alcohol more than once (75 percent of those sixteen to eighteen), and 15 percent felt that their use of alcohol or drugs had ever been a cause of trouble to themselves or others. For 13 percent, alcohol was the problem substance.

If you suspect that you have a problem with drinking, how can you be sure? First, trust your feelings. One of the most reliable indicators of alcohol abuse is the individual's perception of a loss of control. Second, think about your family, your work at school or on the job, and your friends. Are you having difficulties in the areas pinpointed by the RTI studies, and are the people close to you criticizing you for how much you drink? Finally, consider the way you drink. Do you drink at odd hours of the day or when you're alone and attempt to conceal it from those around you? Do you gulp down drinks as if you were thirsty for liquor? Do you drink to make yourself feel better when you're anxious or unhappy, and do you frequently drink just to get drunk?

"There are four questions that have been tested in

adults that best divide people with severe drinking problems from others," points out Dr. Sheila Blume, medical director of Alcoholism and Compulsive Gambling Programs at South Oaks Hospital, Amityville, New York, and former medical director of the NCA. These questions, she says, were devised by Dr. John Ewing of the University of North Carolina, and are called the *CAGE* questions.

- *Cutting down.* Have you ever cut down on your drinking, and if so, why? "If you did it because you're going on a diet, that's one thing, but if you did it because you were getting into some difficulties, that's a warning," says Dr. Blume.
- *Angry or annoyed.* Do you ever feel irritated when people talk to you about your drinking? People with alcohol problems tend to be defensive about them.
- *Guilty.* Have you ever done anything when you were drinking that you were ashamed of later?
- *Eye-opener.* Have you ever had a drink when you first woke up?

These questions are also valid for teenagers, Dr. Blume adds. Few adolescents, however, begin by drinking heavily or every day.

"At first it seems to help with something like shyness," Dr. Blume says, "and so then you use it for anger or to cope with something else, and then you

21

finally just use it. I had a patient who said that when he was young, alcohol made him feel more confident and better about himself. The trouble is that the dose doesn't stay stable. Both the situations in which the person uses alcohol as a remedy and the number of times keeps going up, so the dose goes up, and other problems result.

"Although teenagers may have this progression, many also drink to get drunk and have fun. They don't understand what harm it's doing, they're with a group doing it, and before they know it, they're over their heads and in trouble," Dr. Blume explains.

Jackie, for example, is a fifteen-year-old who drank both to deal with painful feelings and to seem more adult. Both her parents were alcoholics, and she grew up virtually surrounded by liquor. She remembers that when she was a little girl, she would finish all the drinks left on the counter when her parents' parties were over.

"I'd drink until I got drunk and passed out," Jackie recalls. "I'd usually fall asleep on the couch and my father would carry me to bed." Jackie believes that she was drinking four or five drinks at the time, although she doesn't remember feeling sick or hung over later. Her parents, she says, never realized what she was doing.

"I associated drinking with being grown up, and I wanted to be like the grown-ups," she says. When her parents became drunk and fought, she blamed them, not the alcohol.

"I thought they couldn't handle the liquor," she

says, "but that the liquor itself was a good thing." In addition to drinking every two months or so at her parents' parties, Jackie would occasionally sleep over at a friend's house, where the two girls would raid the liquor cabinet.

"When I was about twelve and a half, I started drinking on my own," Jackie continues. "I started cutting school and having blackouts. I would wake up in the morning after parties, and people would tell me things that I did and I didn't believe them."

Jackie made friends with a group of older students who were in their late teens and able to buy liquor for her. She finally reached the point where she was drinking blackberry brandy and whiskey—generally about a pint of alcohol—almost every day. When she did go to school, she would smoke marijuana on her lunch hour. She also mixed alcohol with other drugs. She passed from one grade to the other only because of her high intelligence scores and her mother's explanation to school officials that there was an alcohol problem in the family.

"I was very nervous," Jackie remembers, noting that her alcohol tolerance was increasing all the while. "Once I picked up a drink, I couldn't stop drinking until all the liquor was gone."

Meanwhile, Jackie's parents were breaking up. Finally, when Jackie had been drinking for about two years herself, her mother began attending meetings of Alcoholics Anonymous (AA), a national self-help group. She brought her daughter to some of the meetings, and Jackie began to feel guilty about drinking. She also felt overwhelmed by her problems with school and her parents' marital crisis. When her mother had been sober about nine months, Jackie told her about her own drinking problem. Realizing that her mother was going to send her to a rehabilitation center if she didn't stop, Jackie made a commitment to AA. She also gained insight into her parents' problems by joining Alateen, an AA-affiliated group for children of alcoholics. Jackie has now been alcohol- and drug-free for over a year. In addition to sobriety, she has gained confidence, new friends, a B+ to A average, and an acceptance to the prestigious special high school she always wanted to attend.

Was Jackie's drinking problem typical? There may be as many kinds of teenage problem drinking as there are teenagers who misuse the drug. Certain facts and trends, however, are known about teenagers and alcohol. Here are some points to keep in mind as you read this book:

- *Alcohol is the drug most preferred by teens.* Despite the popularity of marijuana and other substances, alcohol is the drug most widely used by twelve- to seventeen-year-olds in the United States.
- *Among alcoholic beverages, teenagers tend to prefer beer.* Sold in most supermarkets, it is often the easiest drink to obtain. Many teenagers also mistakenly believe that beer in quantity is less harmful than distilled spirits. (In fact, a twelve-ounce can of beer has just as much

alcohol as a mixed drink.) Nor is it true that beer drinkers can't become alcoholics. Jackie's father, for example, is an alcoholic who drinks only beer.

- *Most teenagers have tried alcohol by the time they graduate from high school.* An estimated 85 percent have tried it by tenth grade; over 90 percent by twelfth grade. By the end of high school, nearly two-thirds have actually gotten drunk.

- *The age at which the first drink is taken seems to be decreasing.* Although the mean age for a first drink is about thirteen, many teenagers, like Sandy and Jackie, have been exposed to alcohol when even younger. Moreover, individual alcohol consumption increases throughout high school.

- *Girls are catching up to boys in their drinking.* More boys drink, and drink heavily, than girls do, but studies indicate that the gap is narrowing.

- *Teenagers tend to drink more on a given occasion than people in other age groups.* Although teenagers usually don't drink steadily enough to develop the organ changes seen in adult alcoholics, they're far more likely to suffer from the acute effects of alcohol abuse than adults. Because many are actually drinking to get drunk, they're at high risk for such immediate effects as gastric distress and loss of consciousness, as well as falls, brushes with the law, drunk-driving collisions, and other kinds of accidents.

- *Teenagers who are problem drinkers tend to mix alcohol with other drugs.* This tendency toward *polydrug abuse* has potentially devastating consequences, as the combined effects are usually much more dangerous than the effect of either drug alone. (See Chapter Four.)
- *Teenagers who drink heavily are increasing their risk of developing alcoholism as adults.* Although the majority of teenage problem drinkers seem to mature out of the behavior, a significant proportion (studies have indicated from one-third to one-half) become problem-drinking adults. And because alcohol is an addictive substance, any exposure increases the likelihood of dependency. Some groups—which happen to include all the teenagers mentioned in this chapter—are at special risk. The next chapter will tell you who they are and why.

CHAPTER TWO

Who Becomes an Alcoholic?

"WHEN YOU SEE somebody you really respect and love drinking to excess, it's really hard, and I think drinking myself was the only way I knew of to deal with the pain," says Beth, a twenty-year-old whose father is an alcoholic. "I had tried talking to him a few times to get him to stop, but it never seemed to work. When I drank, it didn't bother me as much.

"The very first time I tasted liquor, I was around five. My father asked me to make him a Scotch and soda, and every time he would ask me to do that, I would sip some on the way back to the living room—and that was pretty weird for a five-year-old. I liked the way it felt going down. But the first time I got drunk, I think I was in seventh grade. I was with two of my girlfriends and we were drinking champagne. We were trying to be grown up.

"My drinking was out of control right away. It seemed that I was drinking a lot as soon as I got into high school. I was always going out with the intention of getting drunk. I felt that I couldn't stop.

ARE YOU DYING FOR A DRINK?

"On weekend parties, at the beginning of my freshman year in high school, I'd split a six-pack of beer with someone. By the end of that year, I'd drink a six by myself. By the time I was a junior, I could drink nine beers and still be walking.

"Right before I went into treatment, I started drinking once or twice during the week as well as weekends. If I went to a party on a school night, I'd try not to drink because I knew if I started, I'd keep going. Then I couldn't get up for school, and that happened about twice a week for two months before I got help. In the summer, though, I'd drink every night and on weekends.

"The most frightening thing that happened to me was waking up and not knowing what had happened the night before, not knowing where I was. One time I woke up in a barn, and I don't know how I got there. When I was fifteen, my sister got married, and I got so drunk I didn't remember the wedding. I never got in an accident, but I was really putting myself in danger. When you're in the car and drunk, you get this feeling of being immortal—as if you could conquer the world. But when I'd wake up in the morning, feeling sick from drinking, I'd think, 'By the grace of God I got home.'"

Other consequences also began to trouble Beth. Her grades in school were poor, only rising to her usual level of A's and B's when she was going through a "dry" spell. She also felt that drinking was taking over what had been a privileged life. Her father was a business executive, her mother was in graduate school, and they had brought up Beth and her siblings in suburban affluence. But even though Beth's father managed to hide his alcoholism and let others in his company run the business (now, she says, he's beginning to be found out), Beth had no cover for her own drinking. The money her parents gave her and that she earned from a part-time job all went to alcohol and drugs (amphetamines and cocaine). Moreover, she was repeating her destructive family patterns in her social life: Her boyfriend, nine years older than she, was also a heavy drinker, who put alcohol above Beth.

"Did you ever have a picture of the way you'd like your life to be?" asks Beth. "Mine didn't fit what was going on. I wanted to be healthy, I wanted to be mature, I didn't want to grow old and look disgusting because of drinking and smoking. I looked at my father once and thought, 'You're going to be just like Dad.' I knew that if I didn't do something, I would grow old and drunk and probably treat my own kids the way I was treated. It was too much of a risk."

At seventeen, Beth began to attend meetings of Alcoholics Anonymous, but felt that she would not be able to make a break from her old crowd without a more structured treatment environment. She turned to her family for help. At first, her parents were astonished by the extent of her problems.

"My father had been 'obliviated' all the time, although he wondered why I came in in the morning sometimes," Beth recalls. "My mother didn't want to believe her little girl was a drunk."

After investigating residential treatment facilities, Beth and her family decided on Parkside Lodge, a private program in the Chicago area, affiliated with Lutheran General Medical Center. When Beth saw the facility, it was her turn to be surprised.

"They showed us the wing for adolescents and I met a few people who were in there," Beth says. "I was really nervous, because I thought they would look like real addicts. I thought, 'I'm going to be with all these tough people and I'm going to be really scared.' But I went in and all the kids looked real normal—they looked like me."

Beth's reaction illustrates one of the most common misconceptions about people who abuse alcohol: that they are usually tough types, skid-row bums who gather in slum doorways, drinking from bottles hidden in paper bags. The reality is that many alcoholics are as successful as Beth's father, and some are celebrities. The people who have been treated for drinking problems in recent years have included former First Lady Betty Ford; actresses Elizabeth Taylor, Liza Minnelli, and Mary Tyler Moore; actor Kiel Martin (who actually played an alcoholic on NBC-TV's "Hill Street Blues"); and such sports stars as baseball's Bob Welch and Darrell Porter, golf's Penny Pulz, and hockey's Derek Sanderson. It's no surprise that the NCA refers to alcoholism as "an equal-opportunity disease."

Another common myth about alcoholism is that there is an "alcoholic personality." While many people claim that they are "addictive types," there is no evidence proving that adult alcoholics are substantially different in character from everyone else. And although teenage abusers do share some personality traits and values (you'll read more about these later), these young people are not an overwhelmingly delinquent group. Despite the heavy correlation between delinquent behavior and alcohol abuse, studies have shown that the proportion of drinkers among delinquents is only slightly higher than the proportion of drinkers in control groups made up of nondelinquent teenagers.

Many people also believe that alcoholics drink because they're severely depressed. Although some people turn to alcohol to relieve unhappiness, lifetime studies have revealed that alcoholics showed significantly higher rates of depression than other people only after they developed the disease. The problems their drinking caused and their lack of control were apparently making them depressed— not the other way around.

"I was put into a psychiatric hospital more or less by my own choice," says Jim, nineteen, who has recovered from his dependency on drugs and alcohol. "I was suicidal—the drugs and the booze were driving me crazy. I was in school with 2,000 people, and I couldn't tell anyone how I felt. I couldn't tell any of the teachers, because I'd get into trouble. By

31

no means could I tell my friends, because they'd laugh at me and wouldn't like me. And I couldn't tell my parents. So I was really stuck. I thought I was going crazy, and my parents were sending me to a psychologist for therapy.

"My therapist thought that I was suffering from depression or some type of psychological problem," Jim says. "I know that a lot of people are diagnosed as being psychologically disturbed when they really have a drug or alcohol problem." It was only after Jim told his parents the truth that he was able to be hospitalized for appropriate treatment.

But if depression and delinquency don't lead to alcohol abuse, what does? And if anyone can become an alcoholic, why doesn't everyone who drinks? To answer these questions, scientists have focused on what makes alcoholics different—why they are less resistant to the disease, why they go beyond the limits most people follow. Here are the factors that seem to play a role.

Cultural Group

Do you know which country has the highest rate of alcoholism? People tend to guess that it's Ireland, but the correct answer is France. The real issue, however, is Northern European ancestry. People from countries in this group—which includes not only France and Ireland, but Britain and the Scandinavian nations—have higher rates of alcoholism than those from other nations. The reason is not climate or birth, but the way these societies view alcohol and its use. In Italy, for example, drinking is not an isolated activity. Alcohol is usually consumed in groups, frequently at the family meal, and in limited amounts. Children learn that there are rules for consumption, and that excessive drinking is frowned upon. In France, alcohol is also consumed in family settings, but public intoxication is accepted. In cultures where refusing a drink is practically unthinkable, where drinking away from home at bars and pubs is encouraged, and where a drunk at a party or on the street is regarded as a harmless fun-lover, rates of alcohol abuse are higher.

Ethnic stereotypes, however, have little to do with an individual's use of alcohol. Drinking practices vary over time, and when people emigrate to a different country, their attitudes toward alcohol may change. It is not nationality itself that is important, but environment.

"I grew up in a German family," says Anna, a recovered adult alcoholic and drug addict. "You'd walk in the door, and it wasn't 'Have a cup of coffee,' but 'Have a beer, have a drink, have a cocktail.' "

In cultures in which stress is high and change is rapid, alcohol may represent relief from pressure. American Indians and young blacks, who face high unemployment and racial discrimination, are at high risk for alcohol abuse.

Biology may also play a small role in the differences in cultural drinking practices. As many as 60 percent of Asians lack a liver enzyme that further breaks down acetaldehyde, the first product released when alcohol is digested. As a result, they frequently become flushed, dizzy, and nauseated after only one drink. This unpleasant side effect may help account for the lower rates of alcoholism in Asian countries.

Finally, among teenagers, religious commitment influences drinking. Teens who report religious involvement have lower rates of alcohol abuse. Among religious teens who do drink, however, those who have alcohol-related problems are more likely to belong to religions that forbid alcohol completely than those that include the use of alcohol on special occasions, such as Communion or Passover. When the prohibition on alcohol is absolute, those who decide to drink have no model for limited use.

This factor does not mean, however, that everyone should "practice" responsible drinking. Availability of alcohol plays an enormous role in the development of alcoholism.

"I'm a firm believer that supply creates demand," says Dr. Ross Brower, assistant professor of public health and psychiatry and assistant attending physician at New York Hospital–Cornell Medical Center, in New York City. "It's hard to be an alcoholic if you have no alcohol. If the culture is such that liquor is in less plentiful supply, alcoholism rates have got to be lower."

Alcoholism in the Family

Physicians have long observed that alcoholism runs in families. Beth's family is a good example: Her father is an alcoholic, and not only Beth but two of her siblings displayed drinking problems at an early age. Sandy, Peter, and Jackie, whom you read about in the first chapter, all have close biological relatives who are alcoholics. Anna's father is an alcoholic, and Jim remembers that both his grandfathers drank excessively.

But although scientists estimate that as many as one-half of alcoholics have an alcoholic parent, they did not understand until recently the nature of the relationship between family history and alcoholism. Were alcoholics raised in alcoholic families just following a bad example, or had they inherited a tendency to the disease?

To answer this question, several researchers studied children of alcoholics who were separated from their parents at birth. The researchers concluded that sons of alcoholics were about four times more likely to develop alcoholism than other children, even if they weren't raised by the drinking parent. Daughters of alcoholics also seemed to be at increased risk, particularly if their mothers had had the disease.

But although these studies indicated a hereditary link, research has not yet revealed how alcoholism is transmitted from one generation to the next. One

35

theory is that alcoholics inherit a higher tolerance for alcohol. From the very first episode, they may report drinking large amounts without suffering the upset stomach, headaches, and hangover that let others know in no uncertain terms that they've overdone it.

Jackie, for example, doesn't remember ever getting sick, despite all the times she drank from the glasses at her parents' parties when she was a small child. Beth's tolerance also developed very quickly, and Sandy found that she got sick only the first time she tried mixing liquors.

"The night before I came into treatment, I drank two six-packs and a quart of whiskey," remembers Bill, seventeen, whose uncle and cousin are both alcoholics. "I did that, and the next day I didn't have a hangover. I got real drunk and I threw up, but I had no hangover. Nothing."

Other research has shown that excessive drinking may not only be less painful for people who have inherited a tendency to alcoholism, it may also be more pleasurable. Although alcohol is a depressant, its first breakdown product, acetaldehyde, is a stimulant. One study showed that sons of alcoholics had more of this chemical in their bloodstreams after drinking than did a control group. They reported feeling more alert and less drowsy than the others. Scientists have also theorized that if children of alcoholics metabolize alcohol differently, they may experience drunkenness in a more pleasurable way than the average drinker, even though the effects on their work, families, and friendships are devastating.

Does this mean that all children of alcoholics should worry about alcoholism? The majority never develop it. For those who do, a variety of factors may be important, including not only heredity but the stresses of growing up in such a family and the poor role model established by the drinking parent or parents. (For more on being a child of an alcoholic, see Chapter Six.)

CHAPTER THREE

Bottled Trouble:
Why Teenagers Drink

Drinking To Feel Better

No one in Fred's family is an alcoholic. But like many adolescents, Fred found that his life was complicated by feelings he couldn't easily handle. After his brother was seriously injured in a car accident, he drank to relieve his anxiety.

"I think it was the need to isolate myself from things," says Fred, a twenty-year-old who began drinking at thirteen. "And the more I drank, the more the problems dissolved. Back then, I wasn't looking at it that way, but now I realize that was really what it was all about.

"I find myself still drinking. I can't put a handle on it because access is so easy. Other things I won't go looking for now, but if I gave it a chance, I would become a true alcoholic.

"Cocaine and alcohol were the two biggest problems I had. Between the two, they really wrecked my life."

Instead of making his problems go away, Fred found that the liquor and drugs intensified his distress.

39

"I became emotionally unstable. I couldn't deal with my feelings—I found myself dwelling on the past and had the weight of the world on my shoulders. It led to sort of a nervous breakdown. I drank and mixed downers, and ended up in a psychiatric hospital. My cousin recommended Daytop," says Fred, who then entered one of the facility's nonresidential programs. "They're teaching me how to deal with my feelings. I've been extremely depressed. I guess it's still anger at the disappointment in myself."

Depression and anxiety aren't the only feelings alcohol may seem to dissolve. Some teenagers also use alcohol to get over shyness and low self-esteem. Beth, for example, was very afraid of dating. Without alcohol, she felt awkward with boys. After a few drinks, it seemed easier to talk and relax. Jackie also found that drinking made her feel more secure, even though the consequences often had the opposite effect.

"I was able not to have any feelings," she says. "It made me more relaxed. I could talk to people—not that I remembered what I said."

Physiological problems may also contribute to drinking. There is some association, for example, between hyperactivity in childhood and adult alcoholism. Some researchers believe that the hyperactive may drink in an attempt at self-medication.

Another theory that has recently been proposed is that many alcoholics are *stimulus augmenters*. This means that any stimulus—a noise or a touch, for example—seems more intense to them than it really is. According to the theory, stimulus augmenters drink to relieve the unpleasantness of hearing every noise at a very loud level or seeing every light as uncommonly bright. One study, in fact, showed a significant incidence of these augmented responses among children of alcoholic fathers. These findings may point to another genetic link in alcoholism. Further research is needed, however, to determine how these perceptual problems are related to alcoholism and what can be done to relieve them.

Drinking "To Have Fun"

Many teenagers drink simply because they believe it will help them enjoy themselves. In the first RTI study, more than 68 percent of the moderate to heavy drinkers considered the social function of drinking ("just to have a good time" and "a good way to celebrate") a very important reason to use alcohol. This was even more important to the drinking teens than a desire to feel better, to be like their friends, or to appear more adult.

Fifteen-year-old Betsy, for example, began drinking at the beginning of the eighth grade. Although she started with only occasional drinks, she soon progressed to drinking every weekend and sometimes on weekdays as well.

"My friends and I would go in the woods and drink

ARE YOU DYING FOR A DRINK?

a whole bottle of hard liquor," she remembers. "We drank whiskey and bourbon. Sometimes, I'd have more than half a bottle by myself. In the summers, we drank really heavily.

"On the weekends, I'd do it to get drunk—I wanted to do it. It made me feel good. Sometimes I'd have a fight with my mother or father and go drink, but mostly I'd do it to have a good time."

After Betsy missed seventy-two classes in one term and began failing, her mother brought her into treatment. One of the hardest obstacles for her to overcome was the belief that she had to have alcohol and marijuana in order to have fun. But now that Betsy has given up alcohol and drugs, she finds that she doesn't really miss drinking with her old crowd.

Expectations like Betsy's—that alcohol will guarantee a good time—influence the way teens experience drinking and whether or not they drink to excess. One recent study of more than 1,500 adolescents, for example, showed that among attitudes, the two most powerful predictors of problem drinking were the belief that alcohol improves thinking processes and coordination (just the opposite is true), and the belief that drinking affects social behavior. The researchers' work also showed that most teens form beliefs like these before they've even had a drink.

Interestingly, such beliefs actually influence the way teens act and feel when they do drink. Studies have proved, for example, that people will behave more aggressively or with less inhibition after they have been given a drink that they're told contains alcohol, even though the glass really contains nonalcoholic tonic water. Similarly, people who have been given alcohol but told that they're getting a soft drink will behave with more restraint than they do when they know they're drinking alcohol. According to this principle, known as the *placebo effect,* most people would have just as much fun drinking soft drinks as alcohol—if they believed that that was all they needed to have a good time.

But although attitudes influence our feelings when we drink, they will not erase the effects of alcohol. Someone who believes drinking will improve driving, for example, may behave as if alert, although the ability to react is really dangerously impaired.

Drinking To Be Like Friends

Most recent studies of teenage drinking show that peer pressure—the sense that others will disapprove of you if you don't follow along—has surprisingly little influence on adolescent use of alcohol. But if friends' disapproval doesn't count, their behavior does. Research shows that teenagers who have drinking friends and who belong to a peer group that encourages drinking are likely to be drinkers themselves. After the RTI studies, the NIAAA concluded that these teenagers were using alcohol because it was the group's means of celebrating and socializing.

"No one forced anything upon me," remembers

Jim. "There were so many people I wanted to be like, that I thought were the really cool people. But I don't think they were responsible. They were just doing their own thing, and that was what I wanted to be like. I succeeded, but I didn't like it once I got there."

Fred, too, went along with drinking not only because it eased his hurts, but because it was part of the fun shared by friends he admired.

"One of them lived across the street," he recalls. "I knew his younger brother—I liked the music they were playing and the whole atmosphere there. And it was easy to drink, because it was so accepted."

But if teenagers drink because their friends do, they also choose other friends because they drink. Teenagers who have problems with alcohol often report that they abandoned their "straight" friends after their drinking got out of control.

Studies have also indicated that *how* teenagers' friends drink—while driving, for instance, or always to get drunk—is just as important in tipping the scale toward problem drinking as the quantity they consume.

"I always hung around with people who were drinkers and druggies," says Jim. "We had the same interests—getting wasted all the time. The friendships I had before fell apart except for one. The other relationships I ruined."

Jim found that he was following a pattern typical of many teens who abuse substances: The behavior reinforced the friendships, and the friendships reinforced the behavior. Like many young people who overcome alcohol or drug problems, Jim discovered that one of the most important steps toward recovery was finding new friends.

"I've had to learn how to reach out with other people," Jim says. "There are so many things that have helped. But it's the fellowship of AA and the friends I've made that have really made the difference."

But why would someone like Jim want to be in a group where alcohol and drugs were the only way to have fun? Although adult alcoholics have personality profiles much like the rest of the population, teenagers who are problem drinkers do differ somewhat from their peers. They tend to be more rebellious, to favor independence over academic achievement, to be more tolerant of unconventional behavior (and to engage in it themselves), and to be closer to their friends than to their parents. Many, in fact, report that their parents were either distant, cold, and uninterested, or so critical and strict that the teenagers couldn't communicate with them. In either case, the group of friends—no matter how abusive their habits—seemed a warmer alternative than the family. And in their quest for independence, many of these young teenagers were precocious. Fred and Jackie, like many drinking teens, had older friends who were more inclined to experiment than their own peers were.

But although personality factors may predispose some teenagers toward alcohol abuse, they are not necessarily an important cause. At times, almost any adolescent will feel rebellious, frustrated, or out of tune with the family. Furthermore, as Jim discovered, alcohol itself can change someone's personality.

"All my interest in sports—Little League baseball, soccer—and all my hobbies stopped," Jim says. "Before, I was usually getting involved with different groups. In eighth grade, I joined the yearbook, and stopped because it was getting in the way of the drinking and drugs."

Drinking To Be Like the Adults

Where do you think most teenagers have their first drink? Contrary to what many believe, American adolescents usually don't have their first sip of liquor at a bar or at a friend's, but at home. It may be in connection with a celebration—say, a taste of champagne with the family on New Year's Eve—or it may be under less pleasant circumstances.

"My mother used to put vodka in my orange juice when I was teething," says Jackie. "I also had beer from my father's glass."

Dan, seventeen, remembers that his alcoholic uncle got him drunk when he was only four.

"I was over visiting him and he was drinking. He said, 'Do you want one?' So we polished off a bottle.

46

When my mother picked me up, she took me home and I got real sick."

Jackie and Dan had liquor when they were too young to know what it was, or to make any choice about its use. Such early experiences, however, have a powerful effect on attitudes toward alcohol. In fact, parents' drinking practices and teenagers' perceptions of their parents' beliefs about alcohol are among the most powerful predictors of teenage drinking styles. If your parents abstain, you're likely to abstain; if they drink, you'll probably drink too. In the second RTI study, for example, only 12 percent of the students who believed that their parents drank regularly were abstainers.

Even more important than parents' drinking behavior, however, is their opinion of teenage drinking. The RTI studies showed that the more the respondents thought their parents approved of teenage drinking, the more they drank. And even though some teens will drink in the face of great disapproval, parental consent—express or implied—is a powerful push toward alcohol.

"My parents used to give us a beer a week at the dinner table. Ever since we were little, they'd give us some," remembers Anne, seventeen. "Now, when I come home drunk, my dad will talk to me. He'll ask me a lot of questions, just to see if I'll mess up. He thinks it's funny."

Whereas some parents, like Anne's, fail to take drunkenness seriously, others find that their teenagers' alcohol abuse fills a need. If, for instance, there are problems in the parents' marriage, an adolescent's drinking can provide relief by giving the warring partners a separate crisis that demands attention. The parents may also wish that the child would remain dependent on them, and an alcohol-dependent teenager is exactly that. The drinking teen may feel, on some level, that he or she is even helping to keep the family together.

Rebecca, sixteen, for example, had many problems with her parents. Although her mother and father are now together, they separated for a while when she was ten. Not long after the separation, her father was sentenced to a prison term for selling cocaine. Rebecca's mother began to drink heavily, and although she would verbally admonish Rebecca not to do the same, her actions carried a different message.

"My mother and father never wanted me to end up like them, but whenever we went out on family things, I was always allowed to have one drink," Rebecca says. "I was about ten at the time—boy, that's young. I was a little manipulator too. I'd say, 'It's just one drink. I won't get drunk.' Then, if I did get drunk, my mother would say, 'You see what happens.' We also had a block party every year on the Fourth of July, and the motive seemed to be to get even more wasted than the year before. I was allowed to drink at those parties. Everybody would get really drunk and be throwing up in my bathroom. My mother would say, 'See what happens.'"

After Rebecca's father left, however, her mother began tacitly to encourage Rebecca's drinking.

"My mother would come home from work and sit down with her bottle of whiskey," remembers Rebecca, now sixteen. "I was drinking myself—my mother made me a kahlua and milk, or let me have beer at parties."

By the time Rebecca was fifteen, she was drinking regularly and mixing the alcohol with marijuana and cocaine. She recalls consuming fifteen beers on an average occasion. In the summer, she drank every night, usually hard liquor. Her scholastic average, which had been in the nineties, eventually plunged because she never went to school. When her parents, who were then back together, found out she had been in high school for only one report card period, they brought her to Daytop Village for treatment.

Although drinking teens like Rebecca often imitate their parents' habits, they frequently report trouble with their families over their alcohol abuse. Parents who are addicted themselves may be genuinely alarmed to see that their children are becoming like them. Parents who don't drink excessively may notice the problem more readily and confront their children. In any case, over 2 million American students—20 percent—were estimated by the RTI researchers to have gotten into trouble with their families over their drinking during the year preceding the second study.

"The only thing I can say," adds Jim, "is that when

I started out doing it, and people tried to tell me how bad it was for you, what it could do to you, I didn't think it was possible—it wasn't going to happen to me. But it did. Adults aren't always wrong. They're not always out to get the kids, and they do care. And if you think you have a problem, you most likely do."

CHAPTER FOUR

Alcohol and Your Body and Mind

Wasted . . . sloshed . . . polluted . . . bombed . . . smashed . . . crocked . . . pickled . . . stewed . . . blitzed . . . dead drunk.

You've probably heard or used most of these slang terms for drunkenness. While some sound humorous, the last has an ominous ring. Can anyone die just from drinking? The answer is yes, and it can happen in several ways.

As you may be aware, alcohol is both a depressant and a poison. A *depressant* is a substance that acts to depress, or slow down, the central nervous system, which governs breathing and heart rates. Someone who has a lethal dose of alcohol—the equivalent of eleven or twelve drinks—may depress the nervous system so much that respiratory and cardiac arrest result. Most heavy drinkers avoid this condition, known as *acute alcohol poisoning,* because they lose consciousness before they can ingest that much alcohol. However, someone who drinks very, very fast may overload on alcohol so quickly that this level is reached before the person passes out. According to the U.S. Department of Health, three people in the United States die from such overdoses every day. One of the more famous cases involved rock musician John Bonham of the once-popular band Led Zeppelin. Bonham died in 1980 after ingesting the equivalent of forty shots of vodka.

Even if someone is lucky enough to pass out before overdosing on liquor, he or she is still not out of danger. Alcohol irritates the stomach lining so much that large quantities frequently cause nausea and vomiting. Someone who vomits while unconscious or groggy may suck food particles into the windpipe. The person will then either choke to death or develop a condition known as *aspiration pneumonia* that arises when foreign bodies enter the lungs. In October 1984, Wells Kelly, the drummer in the backup band for the rock star Meatloaf, was found dead by London police after choking on his own vomit following a heavy drinking bout.

Alcohol also kills in an indirect manner. The vast number of drunk-driving accidents (see Chapter Five) is just one example. According to the NCA, alcohol is a factor in approximately 80 percent of fire deaths, 65 percent of drownings, 70 percent of fatal falls, and up to 40 percent of industrial accidents.

"A girl I know drank a whole bottle of vodka, a whole bottle of blackberry brandy, and then she was drinking beer," says eighteen-year-old Heather. "She got alcohol poisoning. She passed out and smashed her head on a tire. They had to call an ambulance. She had stopped breathing, and was in intensive care for two days. She almost died."

In instances like these, alcohol acts rapidly. But it is a silent killer as well. Although alcoholics can drink for decades and avoid both acute alcohol poisoning and accidents, they can't escape the effects on the brain and other organs, particularly the liver. Later in this chapter, you'll read what some of these changes are, and how they affect teenage drinkers. But first let's examine what happens to Eric, a fictional teenager, during an isolated bout of drinking. Suppose Eric is seventeen years old, that he weighs about 155 pounds, and that he is on his way to a Saturday night party.

When Eric arrives at the party, he's immediately hungry. He skipped dinner earlier, but instead of having a sandwich, he grabs a few salted nuts and decides to have a drink. He knows the host's parents aren't home, and that liquor will be available. He thinks a drink will calm him down—he doesn't feel at ease among people he doesn't know, and the guests are mostly friends of his girlfriend, Susan. She has promised to meet him there, and Eric feels annoyed that she hasn't arrived yet.

With some help from Tony, the host, Eric mixes a whiskey and ginger ale. The salt from the nuts has made him thirsty, and he gulps the drink quickly. Because there is little food in his stomach to slow the absorption of the alcohol, it passes into Eric's bloodstream in less than twenty minutes. Whereas food must be digested further, alcohol is absorbed directly through the stomach wall and the small intestine. The carbonation in Eric's whiskey and ginger ale also helps its passage. Eric isn't aware of this—he only knows that he feels better almost immediately. If one drink can be this good, he thinks, why not have another? In just a few minutes, he gulps a second.

Eric has now been drinking alcohol at a faster rate than his body can metabolize it. In general, it takes someone of average size an hour to an hour and a half to metabolize completely one-half ounce of pure alcohol (ethanol), which is roughly the amount in one drink. Eric has been at the party only half an hour, and he has already had two drinks. He is also feeling the effects. Though he doesn't like to admit it, Eric is an inexperienced drinker and has little tolerance. He is also tired from his weekend job and anxious about his relationship with his girlfriend— factors that can make someone less resistant to alcohol's effects. And he has gulped the drinks on an almost empty stomach—a practice that would make virtually anyone except an alcoholic feel high. And Eric is certainly not an alcoholic.

An hour later, Eric is thoroughly drunk. He has had four drinks rapidly, and the alcohol that his body can't break down is busy coursing through his bloodstream to all his organs. One of the first effects it has on his brain is to anesthetize the part that controls judgment and behavior. As a result, Eric feels freer to say and do what he pleases. So before Susan even gets to the party, Eric has insulted one of her friends.

When Susan arrives, she finds Eric in sorry condition. The alcohol has affected his brain to the point where he has lost both his muscular coordination and his ability to react quickly. On his way to Susan, he stumbles and knocks over a vase on the mantelpiece. Eric tries to catch it, but he's too drunk to stop the fall. It shatters, and Eric stands for a moment in stunned embarrassment. How could he let that happen?

"You're late, Shusan," he mumbles as he reaches her.

"You're drunk!" she hisses. "I don't see how you can embarrass me this way in front of all my friends. Look what you did to Tony's parents' vase! You just better get someone to take you home right now."

"Oh, yeah? Well, I can take care of myself. Who needs you, anyway?"

Eric stumbles away from her and heads back to the liquor. He doesn't feel lighthearted anymore. Maybe another drink? But Eric can't find the whiskey. So he pours some vodka and orange juice into a glass and downs it. Instead of feeling better, he feels terrible. His stomach is horribly queasy and the room seems to be spinning. The more it spins, the worse he feels. He makes a dash for the bathroom, getting there just in time.

But being sick doesn't make Eric feel any better. And the room is still spinning. Maybe he had better stay here awhile. He sinks to the floor. Outside, he hears banging on the door, and Tony's voice. Is that

Susan shouting at him too? He tries to answer, but he can't seem to get any words out. Just then, the room turns black . . .

Eric opens his eyes. He's lying on a bed, fully clothed, but he doesn't recognize the room. A wave of nausea passes over him, and then he remembers. How could he have made such a fool of himself? He looks at his watch and sees that it's 3:30 A.M. Someone must have put him to bed at Tony's. He hopes that they thought to call his parents. "Oh, no," he thinks. "I'm really in for it now."

He lies still. Maybe if he's quiet, the nausea will go away. He tries to think over the events of the evening, but he can't remember them all. He has vague memories of someone shouting at him, but not of being taken upstairs. And what about Susan? They said something to each other, but he can't remember what.

Eric is surprised at his loss of memory, not realizing that such a heavy drinking bout can lead to a blackout. Although blackouts are much more common in alcoholics than in people like Eric, they can and do happen to nonalcoholics because excessive consumption impairs the mechanism in the brain that transfers the memory of events from short-term into long-term storage. Although Eric could remember the conversation with Susan right after it happened, he has lost it several hours later.

Eric sighs. Maybe he should just try to go back to sleep. But even though Eric was tired when he came to the party and hasn't had a full night's rest, he doesn't feel sleepy at all. In fact, he is wide-awake. Although Eric doesn't know it, the alcohol is responsible for his restlessness. He is experiencing what is sometimes called a *rebound effect*. Having been plunged into low gear for some time, his central nervous system is now in overdrive, and Eric feels uncomfortably hyper.

After a couple of hours, Eric goes back to sleep. But when he wakes up in the morning, he's still jittery and nauseated. His head feels as if the Fourth of July fireworks were exploding inside. "Well, at least I know what this is," he thinks. "It's a hangover." What Eric doesn't know, however, is that he is experiencing a mild form of alcohol withdrawal. Eric's isolated experience is just one of the unpleasant realities, magnified many times, that alcoholics live with day after day. And although Eric understandably feels as if he never wants to look at a drink again, an alcoholic would stop that shakiness with a couple of morning drinks—perpetuating the cycle of addiction and dependence.

Eric, fortunately, has only a hangover and some unpleasant social situations to cope with in the morning. He has done his body no permanent damage, and if he avoids episodes like this in the future, his experience with severe intoxication will be no more than a painful memory.

But what if Eric drank more and more, and drank habitually? Here is a summary of the effects on the mind and body of years of alcohol abuse.

Digestive System

Alcohol irritates the throat and stomach lining—the burning sensation you feel if you drink liquor straight will tell you that. But whereas an isolated episode of heavy drinking may cause vomiting, long-term abuse has more devastating effects. The presence of alcohol increases the acidity of the stomach and can lead to a degeneration of its protective lining. A painful and perhaps bleeding ulcer results, all the more dangerous in alcoholics because the clotting ability of their blood is impaired.

The irritating effects of alcohol can lead to other severe conditions. Alcoholics have an increased tendency to develop cancers in their digestive organs and in their mouth and esophagus (the tube carrying food from the mouth to the stomach), particularly if they are also inflaming these areas with cigarette smoke. Their drinking irritates another important digestive organ, the pancreas, leading to an extremely painful and life-threatening condition known as *pancreatitis*. Drinking also places stress on the kidneys.

In addition to organ damage, alcoholics frequently suffer from malnutrition, a condition that begins with the alcoholic's life-style. Because alcohol is a fluid filled with calories (there are about eighty-two in a half-ounce of pure alcohol), the drinker feels full after consuming several drinks. But because these

are "empty" calories (liquor has virtually no nutrients), the drinker has failed to get the important
substances needed for good health. In addition,
many alcohol abusers are so caught up in their
drinking—or so nauseated from its effects—that they
don't even think about food.

"You wouldn't eat and you'd drink," says fifteen-
year-old Betsy, recalling her own experiences with
alcohol abuse. "But you wouldn't miss eating."

But even if a heavy drinker makes a point of eating
normally, the irritated digestive system can't function
effectively to absorb the nutrients needed. Furthermore, alcohol itself impedes the absorption of certain nutrients, including a number of vitamins, and
blocks the effects of others.

Liver damage is another important reason why
alcoholics suffer malnutrition. This vital organ, frequently referred to as the body's furnace, is responsible for converting a number of food substances into
usable components for building and repairing cells. It
is also the organ primarily responsible for breaking
down alcohol.

Just what does alcohol do to the liver? First, it
interferes with the process by which we maintain a
normal level of blood sugar. When alcoholics drink
and don't eat, their blood sugar level can dip dangerously low, leading to confusion, light-headedness,
and sometimes loss of consciousness. Anna remembers that she used to get up in the morning and drink
cordials and sweet liqueurs. She realizes now that her
blood sugar was probably low, and she was attempt-

ing to satisfy her need for sugar at the same time that she was pursuing her addiction to alcohol.

Alcohol also disrupts the liver's normal metabolism of fats, which leads to the condition known as *cirrhosis*. When someone drinks heavily, the liver will burn alcohol instead of fat. Other biochemical changes actually bring fat from other parts of the body to the liver. Fat deposits accumulate, leading to a condition known as *fatty liver*. This is a correctable problem if the person stops drinking. If alcohol abuse continues, however, the victim develops what is known as *alcoholic hepatitis*. The liver cells become severely inflamed and some of them die. This life-threatening condition inhibits the ability of the liver to manufacture digestive chemicals and to cleanse the circulatory system of dead red blood cells and certain toxic substances. Finally, if the person continues to drink, cirrhosis develops. The liver becomes filled with hard, bumpy scar tissue instead of healthy cells. At this stage, there is no hope of recovery. And because no one can survive without at least minimal liver function, cirrhosis is frequently fatal. It is a major cause of death in the United States (according to the NCA, some 30,000 deaths a year are attributable to cirrhosis), and it is largely preventable: Very few nonalcoholics die of cirrhosis.

Do teenagers suffer from cirrhosis? In general, the answer is no, because cirrhosis usually takes anywhere from five to twenty-five years of severe alcohol abuse to develop. But as people abuse alcohol at earlier ages, physicians are reporting seeing younger patients with evidence of the disease. And teenagers are certainly subject to the reversible damage that, if unchecked, can lead to cirrhosis. Young drinkers are often not aware of this, because liver disease in its early stages is painless. Nor is it necessary to get drunk all the time to develop it. Scientists have done experiments on volunteers who consumed six drinks over the course of a day without ever reaching the blood-alcohol level at which they would be considered intoxicated. Nonetheless, they all showed signs of fatty liver after about three weeks of drinking at this level.

"You can get acute alcoholic hepatitis from short-term binge drinking," points out Dr. Ross Brower. "But that's usually something you wouldn't be able to discern from a hangover."

One teen who developed hepatitis is Kathy, now twenty. Between the ages of twelve and seventeen, Kathy drank steadily and also abused other drugs. By the time she was fifteen, she would drink three six-packs or a half-quart of straight alcohol by herself. The morning after a three-day bout of drinking, Kathy was finally sober at home and tried to eat breakfast. She felt so sick and dizzy that she was rushed to the hospital. Tests later revealed that she had hepatitis. Kathy doesn't know if she developed the condition from drinking or from the few occasions that she used a needle to inject drugs.

"I did a lot of damage to myself physically—my nerves and my liver," remembers Kathy, who no longer drinks. "I remember going to a doctor and having him tell me that my liver was all screwed up. The idea of ever having hepatitis again scares me —getting it a second time could be fatal. I care more about my body now."

Heart and Circulatory System

Through biochemical changes and malnutrition, alcohol weakens the heart muscle and impairs its ability to pump. This condition, called *alcoholic cardiomyopathy,* is extremely dangerous. Although it usually affects older alcoholics, heart irregularities can also occur in young drinkers. One of these conditions, nicknamed *holiday heart,* consists of fluttery feelings and irregular heartbeats. While these are not dangerous in a teenager with a normal heart, those who binge can develop *myocarditis,* a potentially serious inflammation of the heart muscle. Kathy, who was an extremely heavy drinker and probably a young alcoholic, remembers that she frequently had heart palpitations and stabbing pains in her chest during the time of her alcohol and drug abuse.

Alcohol also affects the heart indirectly. Because the liver is not burning fat, there is an excess of fat in the blood. A high concentration of certain fats is a predisposing factor in heart attacks. Alcohol also raises blood pressure. When the liver becomes clogged with fat and scar tissue, the normal circulatory pathways into and out of the organ are blocked.

Veins in other parts of the body, especially the esophagus, swell as the blood seeks alternate routes. These veins, called *varices*, can rupture, causing massive and frequently fatal bleeding.

Brain and Central Nervous System

If alcohol is abused over a long period of time, it affects the membranes surrounding the brain cells, interfering with their ability to transmit information. Eventually, however, the brain cells adapt, and the membranes harden and become more resistant to alcohol's effects. This reaction may help explain alcoholics' high tolerance and their ability to drink large quantities of liquor without appearing drunk. The danger, however, is that their brain cells have adapted so much to alcohol that alcoholics can't function normally in its absence. This is what causes withdrawal.

As an alcoholic continues to abuse alcohol over time, brain cells die and certain functions are impaired. The most severely affected are those relating to visual and spatial abilities, short-term memory, abstract reasoning, and problem solving. Alcoholics have particular trouble with learning situations that require them to process new information rapidly. In severe alcoholics, the brain can actually atrophy, or decrease in size.

What does this mean for teenage drinkers? Although young people who abuse alcohol usually don't show the extensive brain damage sometimes seen in older alcoholics, they may suffer from less obvious impairment. When tested, they show deficits in attention span, abstract reasoning, and memory. And while the capacity to recover learning abilities seems greater in younger alcoholics than in older ones, there is no guarantee that the brain can compensate for what has been lost.

Jim, for example, once a good student, failed most of his classes after he became involved with alcohol and drugs. Although he finished in the top third of his class and went on to college after he attained sobriety, he feels that his learning capacity hasn't fully recovered.

"I'm doing rather well, but I think if I'd never gotten involved with the drugs and the alcohol, I would be a better student," he says. "It's changed my ability to learn and to absorb information. It's definitely a lot better than when I first got out of treatment. Back then, I wouldn't have been able to carry on a conversation like this—my mind would have wandered. But I still have to force myself to listen if I'm in class."

Alcohol has another effect that is important to consider. Whereas many people think that alcohol makes them sexier, its physiological action is quite the reverse. In males, heavy drinking results in a decrease in production of the male hormone testosterone, and prolonged alcohol abuse can even cause a reduction in size of the testicles. Alcohol abuse has also been associated with menstrual irregularities in women. If a woman is pregnant, the consequences are devastating. You may have read warnings of the possible adverse effects of alcohol consumption during pregnancy. This is because alcohol—even in small amounts—can reach the developing fetus through the woman's bloodstream. Its effects on the infant range from low birth weight and small head size to growth deficiencies, heart and brain abnormalities, and mental retardation. Prolonged alcohol abuse can lead to stillbirths or full-fledged fetal alcohol syndrome (FAS). FAS includes all the abnormalities listed, plus joint and facial anomalies. It is now considered the third leading cause of birth defects—and the only one that is completely preventable.

Because even small amounts of alcohol can harm the fetus, most doctors now advise women to drink no liquor at all during pregnancy. Women are even asked to abstain while they are trying to conceive. Abstinence is necessary because alcohol ingestion seems to be especially harmful in the early stages of fetal development, when a woman may not even be aware that she is pregnant.

Alcohol also carries special risks for teenagers. Whereas the chronic effects of heavy drinking—such as cirrhosis—usually take years to develop, a single episode that culminates in a traffic accident, a fall, a drowning, or an overdose can wipe out a teenager's future in an instant.

"I had a friend who was killed—he lived across the street from me," says Jim. "He was in an accident, and the kid who was driving was drunk. That was my freshman year. I think it had an effect on me for about a week. I didn't think anything of it in relation to myself. I wasn't afraid. I'm more concerned now than I was then. The booze and drugs made me feel that I was Superman and I could handle anything. I could see others had a problem, but I couldn't see it happening to me."

Another problem that seems to affect teenagers is a rapid descent into alcohol dependence. Whereas the number of adolescents who are clinically alcoholic may be small, many professionals believe that those who become alcoholic develop the addiction at a faster rate than adults.

"Adults who drink adhere to certain social controls in regard to the use of the drug—you don't drink before 5 P.M.; you don't drink by yourself— various little rules that most adults, even problem drinkers, try to adhere to," points out Dr. Brower. "Adolescents don't have that. Kids are not concerned with the time, and they're not necessarily drinking in social situations. They're drinking to get drunk, for the effect of it. There are no controls whatsoever, and the addiction progresses more rapidly because the factor in dependency is consistent use. Kids drinking every day develop it quickly.

"The other reason I think adolescents get into trouble is because they may use alcohol to handle emotional problems, and they're not aware of other ways to cope," Dr. Brower adds. "Their peers may look down upon counseling. Adults, on the other hand, are generally more likely to seek some kind of help."

Kathy, for example, felt painfully shy when she was growing up. Usually the butt of teasing from her older brothers, Kathy tried to find ways to make them like her—which included drinking with their friends and selling marijuana for them. Having started drinking at age twelve, Kathy was heavily involved with both drugs and alcohol by the time she entered junior high school. Jim also began drinking at eleven or twelve. Once he was in high school, he began planning his entire day around alcohol and drugs.

"I couldn't function unless I was high. I couldn't deal with people, and I'd get really nervous if I wasn't under the influence of something. It was at the point where I had to get high every day before I went to school," Jim says.

"I'd get up and have a little bit to eat, and if I had pills—usually downers—I'd take a couple of those," he recalls. "I'd go to the bus stop and smoke three or four joints, and maybe someone would have a bottle. We'd drink a couple of beers or have a bottle of wine. Then we'd get to school rather early and smoke some more pot and go to our classes. About 10, I'd duck out to the bathroom and smoke another joint. I didn't drink in school that much, because I was afraid of getting caught. Then at lunch, I'd get high. As soon as I got home from school, someone would have a case of beer, and we'd sit around and get high and drink. Then I'd come home for dinner, act really cool, and go out after dinner and do the same thing. I'd come home on time, but then I'd lock myself in my room and get really high and pass out. I was under the influence twenty-four hours a day."

Such heavy abuse not only damages the mind and body, but interrupts emotional growth. Jim, for example, had to repeat his junior year in high school. Repeating was necessary to salvage his scholastic standing, and, he says, because "I had to grow up." Teens who continue to drink into their twenties, however, often find that they are adults only in the chronological sense. Among the emotional areas most severely affected by alcohol abuse, clinicians point out, are the capacity to form attachments and the ability to attain independence.

Twenty-year-old Fred, for instance, feels that one of the reasons he's now depressed is because "I lost a couple of years out of my childhood." Anna feels that she never grew up until she entered treatment.

"I lived in the here-and-now and the instant," she says. "I never planned. I really feel like I grew up in my thirties. It wasn't until my late twenties or early thirties that I even owned a watch. I just hated the word *time*. If someone said, 'You'll feel better in time,' my attitude was, 'The hell with it. I want to feel better now.'"

Alcohol compounds emotional immaturity in another way too. Because alcohol tends to release inhibitions and to impede judgment, its abuse can lead to erratic moods and sometimes to violent behavior. People frequently refer to alcohol as "dissolving" the conscience, and this effect is well-documented by statistical studies showing that more than 50 percent of homicides are alcohol-related, as are perhaps as many as 90 percent of reported child abuse cases. While not all heavy-drinking teens become violent, alcohol aggravates the mood swings and changing feelings that are a normal part of growing up.

"Like they say, with drinking you get nine different personalities," says Sandy. "I did some sick things when I was drinking heavily. I used to rip up clothes, throw things away, carve the furniture. I'd come in late all the time or I wouldn't come in at all. I ran away. And I got into many fights with people."

Kathy remembers that she was repeatedly violent when she was abusing alcohol and drugs. Her dangerous behavior ranged from hitting and kicking friends to tossing a bottle at her mother and, on another occasion, throwing a chair at her when she arrived at the police station where Kathy was being held for drunk driving. Dan vandalized a bus when he was drunk; Bill got into fistfights with his best friends.

Teens risk harming themselves as well as others. The depressant effects of alchohol can be especially devastating to someone who already feels inadequate and out of control because of alcohol dependence. This can lead to suicidal feelings and behavior. Alcoholics are at greater risk for suicide than the rest of the population, and the NIAAA deems alcohol a factor in 25 to 37 percent of suicides nationally.

Anna came close to being one of those statistics. One Memorial Day weekend, debilitated from a constant cycle of taking uppers and downers, she decided on a brief vacation to restore her spirits. She went first to her parents' house, intending to pick up some summer clothes. (Though in her thirties at the time, Anna had been living with her parents until shortly before this incident.) Knowing that her parents were out of town and wouldn't be aware of her behavior, she decided to have a few drinks before leaving.

"My resistance to everything, any substance, was down at that point," Anna recalls. "And the next thing I knew, I was in the medicine chest looking for a nice, clean razor, and I literally ripped my neck open. I left a suicide note and I lay down on my bed, back in the room I had as a little girl. I took a towel with me because I didn't want to mess up the bedspread. And I didn't go there thinking I was going to do it—I went there to get summer clothes, and I snapped. After I had a few drinks, that was it. I was so tired, I just couldn't go on any more. I had no energy left."

Fortunately, Anna had inadvertently taken her sister's apartment key with her to her parents' house. Her sister came to the house and found Anna, weak from loss of blood and barely conscious.

Kathy also tried suicide by slashing one of her wrists when she was sixteen. Her parents broke down the bathroom door before she could seriously injure herself. Although she isn't sure whether her attempt was a cry for help or a genuine effort to kill herself, Kathy remembers being flooded with self-hatred. "I had no self-worth at all," she says. "I felt I had no friends and no one cared about me."

Double Jeopardy: Alcohol and Other Drugs

Although both Anna and Kathy made conscious efforts to harm themselves, they could have succeeded in committing suicide unintentionally by combining alcohol with other substances. This habit is frequently seen among teenagers, who are what the NCA calls *polydrug abusers.* In the 1984 Gallup survey, for example, 21 percent of the sixteen- to eighteen-year-olds said that they had combined alcohol with another drug. "This can lead to new and more horrible effects than those of just alcohol or drugs alone," points out Dr. Sheila Blume.

Downers such as barbiturates (sleeping pills) and tranquilizers, for example, have very powerful effects on a drinker. Those who abuse alcohol will have a tolerance for these substances and for narcotics (painkillers) even if they don't take them habitually. This phenomenon, called *cross-tolerance,* occurs because these substances share certain characteristics with alcohol and affect the mind and body in similar ways. An alcohol abuser would have to take several of these pills to feel high, just as he or she would require more drinks than the average person to feel drunk. But although a person becomes tolerant to

71

some of the sedative effects of the drug, its ability to depress the respiratory system is unaltered. And since narcotics and tranquilizers are powerful depressants, what seems enough to be pleasurable can easily become too much.

The situation is doubly dangerous if the person taking the downers is already drunk. Increased tolerance doesn't operate in this instance because both substances require the same organ systems to break them down. If your liver is trying to metabolize both alcohol and a tranquilizer, the effects of both will be in your system for a longer time. Even more dangerous is the tendency for these effects to be additive. Because your central nervous system is being depressed by more than one substance simultaneously, it takes far less of either chemical to kill you. Sometimes the two substances interact so that the effects are not only added together, but multiplied. This formula is responsible for countless deaths, including that of actress Marilyn Monroe; no one knows if she intended to kill herself.

Jean, nineteen, remembers ingesting a potentially lethal combination of pills and alcohol.

"We went on a school trip to an amusement park," Jean says. "The teacher knew I was smacked. I couldn't walk straight and I was sick. They had to rush me to the hospital because I couldn't breathe right."

Whereas downers magnify the depressant effects of alcohol, amphetamines, or *uppers*, counteract them. This action, however, is limited, and can give the abuser a false sense of security. The speed or uppers will increase alertness but will do nothing to combat the loss of motor ability and reduction in reaction time that accompanies drinking. Someone who has taken both will feel as if he or she is performing up to par, when in fact performance is seriously impaired.

Stimulant drugs, such as speed and cocaine, also tend to be shorter-acting, points out Dr. Brower.

"You walk around thinking the balance is okay, and suddenly you're on your face," he says. "It seems to be a frequent cause of automobile accidents —the stimulant effect wears off, and you're suddenly hit by the sedative effect of the alcohol."

Kathy almost died from this combination. After a Halloween party at which she had taken speed and drunk straight whiskey, she came home and started to draw water for a bath. She got in the tub, and the next thing she knew, she was waking up in bed. Her father and brother told her that they had heard water running and broke down the bathroom door. When they got in, Kathy was unconscious—and the water was up to her nose.

Alcohol can also have an additive effect when taken with marijuana and hallucinogenic drugs. In combination with marijuana, it can cause nausea and increase the impairment of motor coordination and distortion of time and space. Teens who have taken alcohol with hallucinogens or with a wide variety of drugs have reported unpredictable and terrifying effects.

73

"I OD'd once," says Joann, fifteen. "I started off with a six-pack of beer and then did some dust [angel dust, the street name for phencyclidine, or PCP, a powerful hallucinogen]. Then I did about three ups and took a hit of acid. It was a real hot day in the summer. My friends were swimming in somebody's backyard pool and I was just lying in the sun. When my friends got out of the pool, they were real worried—I just didn't move. One of them finally got me to come to. I was feeling real sick. I thought I'd pass out again, and I couldn't walk straight. One of them stuck a finger down my throat and I threw up all over the backyard. They took me in the house and gave me some milk, but that made me throw up more. I didn't go to the hospital, but I probably should have. I was sick for a couple of days. That was one of the times that I told myself I'd stop."

Joann and the other teenagers in this chapter suffered no permanent harm. For young people who have not been drinking for many years, the physical effects of alcohol abuse are largely reversible—*if* they survive to stop drinking. Hector Del Valle almost didn't.

CHAPTER FIVE

Hell on Wheels: Drinking and Driving

ON THE EVENING OF September 17, 1982, seventeen-year-old Hector Del Valle was in the mood to celebrate. Two acquaintances had just spent a week putting fancy wheels and decorations on Hector's newly purchased 1972 Ford Maverick, and installing the car's $250 stereo system. Hector's girlfriend wanted to go out to dinner to toast the work's completion, but Hector said no—he owed his helpers a case of beer.

When Hector arrived at the boys' house, they suggested he take the car for a test drive. While he was out, Hector met two girls he knew. He had helped renovate the apartment one of them rented, and she also wanted to pay with a gift of liquor: If he had the time, why not come out for a drink? Using his fake ID, Hector bought a bottle of Amaretto liqueur and a six-pack of beer. He spent the evening at the girl's apartment, drinking heavily. At 11, he proposed that they all get in his car and head for a nearby pizza place.

They never got there.

"I woke up in the hospital with screws in the sides of my head," Hector recalls. "My body was on a striker frame, and every two hours they would come in and turn me, just like they'd turn a pig on a spit. When I got out of that, I had no movement in my body at all. I was actually paralyzed from the neck down, and I was in shock, and the only thing I could feel at the time was the pillow under my head."

Despite his critical injuries, Hector remembered what happened. While heading east in the left lane on Route 46 in Dover, New Jersey, he decided to pass the car in front of him. The other driver, however, didn't move over. Hector, drunk and impatient, decided to pass him on the right, a dangerous (and in most states illegal) move. But Hector was too intoxicated even to know his right from his left.

"I got really confused and went in my left lane," Hector says. "But I didn't have a left lane—just the other side of the highway." Within seconds, Hector had hit two oncoming cars and smashed into a brick wall. The Ford that he bought with his own money, that he "treasured more than anything else," was a twisted wreck, so grossly misshappen on the driver's side that emergency crews had to use special equipment to cut it open. Miraculously, the other eight people involved in the accident were unhurt. But Hector's neck had been broken by the impact, and his spinal cord was injured.

"I should have died," Hector says. "I should have died on the way to the hospital, but something kept me going." After desperate efforts to stabilize him at Dover General Hospital succeeded, Hector began on a six-month road to recovery.

"Time just went by," he remembers. "One day, they told me that I wouldn't be walking right away, that I was paralyzed, and that I would be going to a rehabilitation center. I thought that maybe things would change when I got there."

Hector did regain movement in his arms and some feeling in the lower half of his body, but his legs failed to respond. Finally, one of the doctors told him that he would never walk again. Two others said they weren't sure—the fact that Hector has sensation in his legs is encouraging, but doesn't necessarily mean that he will regain movement. Hoping that he will walk again, throughout years of extensive therapy and an operation to replace the shattered bone in his spine, Hector has been living "one day at a time.

"Before my accident, I used to live for today, but I used to want to get high, and then worry about what I was going to do tomorrow, tomorrow," Hector explains. "I guess you could say that I'm living differently now. I have a lot more faith than before, and I see myself walking in the future."

But at the present time, Hector is a quadriplegic, confined to an electric wheelchair. He has full use of his arms and partial use of his hands, but his fingers and his body below the shoulders are still paralyzed. Hector, however, prefers to concentrate on what he can do rather than what he can't. Through persever-ance, exercise, and the use of special equipment,

Hector is self-sufficient, requiring help only when he goes to bed. He drives again, using a van outfitted with hand controls. He has also completed his high school education, and has taken courses in philosophy and religion at a local community college.

"When I got out of the hospital, I said, 'I don't want to change everything,'" Hector says. "I wanted to go back to school, because I'd be busy from 9 to 3, and able to live my own life. I wanted the burden on me, not my girlfriend or my family. I gave a speech at my graduation about what happened to me, and Channel 2 picked it up, and ever since, my story's gone nationwide. And now people talk about the kid in the wheelchair who's taking his accident so well. I guess that's what I'm doing. I took something really terrible and tried to make it into something positive."

Hector's courage and optimism help him focus on the future rather than on the life he had before the accident. Back then, Hector was not only an enthusiastic dancer, but a gymnast who would probably have been captain of his high school team if he hadn't been injured. And even though his relationship with his family and girlfriend have been strengthened throughout his recovery, many of his old friendships have suffered.

"The friends I used to go dancing with and go out and play football with don't hang around as much," Hector says, "because when we do see each other, we just sit there and talk about good old times. Sometimes I feel like I died, or our friendship died, in that accident, and they just have good memories of me now."

One of Hector's most important efforts today is educating other teens to the hazards of drinking and driving. Shortly after his graduation, he began giving talks in high schools throughout New Jersey. He now has a full-time job as public relations adviser to the Bergen County office of the NCA. He has another job selling insurance, and is coordinating a nonalcoholic nightclub for young people in his hometown. CBS-TV is also planning to air a television movie based on his story.

"I thought something like this would never happen to me," Hector says, "and that's what my story is all about, because that's what a lot of students are saying to themselves. I've talked to over 25,000 seniors, and I see a lot of faces looking at me and saying, 'Oh, that could never be me. I would *die* if that happened to me.' And yet they drink and drive. I met people in the hospital who were probably saying that. And I know what it's like to say, 'That could never happen to me.'"

Ironically, Hector had that belief even though he had already been a victim long before his crippling accident. When Hector was about seven years old, his uncle was driving him to a family dinner when their car was struck by a drunk driver. No one was seriously hurt, and Hector's only memory of the accident was that the damages his family collected enabled him to own his first bicycle.

"Drinking and driving was never brought up to me

as 'No, that's a bad thing, don't do it,' " Hector says. "It was, 'Do it if you want to, but don't get caught.' "

Hector's experiences with drinking began much earlier than his teens. In the fifth grade, he was caught bringing a pitcher of wine on a school field trip and was suspended for three days. At the time, he would go to the houses of friends whose parents were heavy drinkers and have a beer in the basement every few weeks. By the time he was sixteen, he was smoking pot heavily and getting drunk on weekends.

"I thought I was more of a responsible drinker because I drank only on weekends," he says. "But when I drank, I drank for only one reason: to get drunk. I did it for the high—to feel better than I did working a job long hours. It was mostly at a party. But if there wasn't a party, I would really go berserk —I probably drank even more. And that's what happened the night of my accident. There was no party to go to, and I just drank myself dry."

Teenage males like Hector are much more likely to be involved in alcohol-related crashes than their female peers. Girls, however, are not immune to the drinking and driving problem. Page, a nineteen-year-old from a small town north of New York City, has had two frightening experiences, one of which ended in tragedy. The first time, she, like Hector, failed to connect what happened with alcohol.

"Two of my friends were in a car accident three years ago because they were drinking," she says. "I'd just gotten out of the car. They were bringing me back from this party, and they let me and my girlfriend off in front of my house. We heard them racing up and down the road, and we went back up the street to see what was going on. That's when we saw the accident—they were speeding and hit a telephone pole." Page's friends, sixteen and eighteen, were killed instantly.

"I never thought at the time, 'If they weren't drunk, they wouldn't have gotten into the accident,'" Page says. Two and a half years later, Page herself was behind the wheel drunk.

"I was at a party and got really drunk, and after that, I went to a bar," she says. "I'd left with a friend, and I had to help him—he was really, really trashed. I planned to bring him to a diner or something. We started driving and only went about a mile, but I did a lot of things wrong. I was swerving, I ran a stop sign, and I pulled a wide turn. The next thing I knew there were these flashing lights out of nowhere. The cop pulled me over, got me out of the car, and frisked me."

Page, who was driving a friend's car, was arrested for driving while intoxicated and operating a motor vehicle without a license. The results of her test for blood/alcohol concentration (BAC—the percentage of a person's total blood volume by weight that is alcohol) was .14—.04 above the level that the law deems intoxication. After several court appearances, Page was ordered by a judge to pay a $250 fine, go through an education program for drunk drivers, and attend four meetings of AA. The classes, Page says, convinced her to curb her drinking.

"I stopped because I learned so much about it," she says. "It was a really powerful course—it really sank in."

According to numerous studies, Hector's and Page's experiences are all too frequent in the United States. Statistics from the National Highway Traffic Safety Administration (NHTSA) in Washington, D.C., show that alcohol is involved in over 50 percent of the fatal crashes that occur each year. In early 1984, another study was released by the American College of Pathologists in Chicago. This research, based on reports from medical examiners, put the figure even higher, implicating drunk drivers in close to 90 percent of fatal accidents. The study showed alcohol is also involved in close to a quarter of the crashes that result in serious injury but no deaths.

Here are some sobering statistics from the NHTSA:

- One out of two Americans will be involved in an alcohol-related traffic accident in their lifetime.
- More than 700,000 people are injured every year in alcohol-related accidents, 74,000 of them seriously.
- Drunk driving costs American taxpayers an estimated $21 billion to $24 billion each year in hospitalization, legal fees, lost work time, and related expenses.
- In the time it takes you to finish reading this chapter, someone, somewhere, will have died in an alcohol-related crash.

Unfortunately, teenagers play a significant role in this grim statistical picture. According to the NHTSA, teenagers are two and a half times as likely to be in a fatal crash involving alcohol as the average driver. And even though sixteen- to twenty-four-year-olds make up only 20 percent of the total population of licensed drivers, the drinkers among them account for almost half (42 percent) of fatal alcohol-related accidents in the United States. According to the NCA, the result is 5,000 teenagers killed each year and 130,000 injured in drinking/driving crashes.

It is also important to remember that not all dead or injured young people were responsible for the accidents involved. Candy Lightner, the woman who founded Mothers Against Drunk Drivers (MADD), a citizen activist group that lobbies for tougher laws and penalties against drunk drivers, lost her thirteen-year-old daughter, Cari, in 1980 to an intoxicated driver who had twice been convicted of the offense and was out on bail after a third arrest. Cari wasn't even in a car—she was struck from behind as she walked to a church picnic. Cari was counted as one of an estimated 8,514 innocent victims (innocent in that they had not been drinking) killed that year.

Why do teen drivers have such a disproportionate number of problems with alcohol? According to Charles Butler, manager of driver education programs for the Automobile Association of America (AAA) in Falls Church, Virginia, teenagers have little lifetime experience with drinking and just as little experience with driving.

"There are two things that very many people don't know about drinking. The first is that the only real countermeasure to intoxication is time," points out Mr. Butler. "Your body, on average, processes one drink in approximately one hour and fifteen minutes. The other thing people don't realize is that a drink is a drink is a drink. That is, a twelve-ounce can of beer, a five-ounce glass of wine, and a one-ounce shot of whiskey are equal—they have the same alcoholic content, and they all pack the same punch."

In most states, the blood alcohol concentration at which a person is judged by law to be intoxicated is .10. This does not mean, however, that it's safe to drive as long as your BAC is less than that. Most state laws define someone with a BAC of half that amount (.05) as *impaired,* which means that while such a driver is not legally drunk, he or she has ingested enough alcohol to be dangerously affected. Even accidents involving drivers with BACs ranging from .01 up to .049 are described as *alcohol-involved.* Not surprisingly, the risk of an accident increases as BAC increases. Studies have shown that the risk of being responsible for a crash at a BAC of .10 varies from approximately three times as great to almost fifteen times as great as the risk for someone whose BAC is zero.

If these are the factors involved, how much alcohol

is too much? Research sponsored by the Insurance Institute for Highway Safety, in Washington, D.C., proves that people make mistakes performing experimental tasks at BACs as tiny as .015. Teens seem to be particularly vulnerable at low concentrations. Although they actually drink and drive less than adults, they are much more likely to be involved in accidents at even low and moderate BACs. In fact, drivers between sixteen and twenty-four have the highest rate of alcohol-related crashes for any age group, and such accidents are the leading cause of death for this age group in the United States.

If you're more at risk from the effects of drunk driving, what can you do to prevent it? First, never drive after drinking. While this sounds obvious, in the 1984 Gallup Survey of Teenage Attitudes Towards and Use of Alcohol and Drugs, a quarter of those polled reported that they had driven a car shortly after having had a drink. Data from the RTI studies indicated that more than half a million teenagers nationwide had driven after having "a good bit to drink" ten or more times during the previous year.

If you are ever tempted to drive in that situation, remember the alternatives: Get a sober friend to drive you home, call a cab for you, or let you sleep over. If a friend has been drinking, make the same arrangements for him or her. You may even have to take away your friend's car keys, but chances are that you'll both be grateful later. Remember that one of the mottoes of SADD (Students Against Driving Drunk, a group you'll read more about later) is "Friends don't let friends drive drunk."

Another important rule is to drive defensively. Just because you're not drunk doesn't mean that you're safe from drivers who are. (That's one out of ten on an average weekend night.) Always wear a safety belt—they substantially reduce the risk of death and serious injury in collisions. You can also make it a point to keep driving at night (between 8 P.M. and 6 A.M.) to a minimum. These are the most dangerous hours for all drivers, and especially for youths. Finally, if you see a driver on the road who appears to be drunk, alert the police. This practice has been implemented as part of a very successful program in Nebraska called REDDI (Remove Drunk Drivers Immediately), in which citizens use CB radios to report intoxicated motorists.

Legislative changes are another important means to combat drunk driving. Groups like SADD, MADD, and RID (Remove Intoxicated Drivers, based in Schenectady, New York) lobby continually to get state and local legislators to institute stiffer penalties against drunk drivers. These range from higher fines and license suspension (or revocation for repeat offenders) to mandatory jail sentences. Many citizen activist groups also favor higher liquor taxes, which help make alcohol prohibitively expensive.

Certain legal proposals affect teens directly. One of these is the move to establish a national minimum drinking age of twenty-one. Various studies show that states that raise the drinking age experience an average decline of 28 percent in accident fatalities in the age group affected by the law. (Fatalities go up a comparable percentage when states lower the drinking age, as a number did in the early 1970s.)

Other proposals that affect young people concern laws that raise the age at which they can obtain a driver's license. Nighttime curfews for young motorists have also lowered fatality rates.

Interestingly, although teens in overwhelming numbers might be expected to oppose such measures, the Insurance Institute for Highway Safety's 1983 survey of 50,000 public high school students indicated that almost half supported some restrictions on teenage driving. The majority, in fact, favored curfews and mandatory seat belt use.

Another effective weapon against drunk driving is education—not just rehabilitative courses such as the one Page took, but programs that emphasize prevention. Some of the most innovative in the United States were developed and/or run by teenagers themselves. Five such programs are described here. (For program addresses, see the Appendix.)

SADD

The SADD movement began as an outgrowth of MADD, the group you read of earlier. Its purpose is to mobilize students to help each other. Kim Ritchie, a young Virginian, started a SADD group at her school in 1982 after a fellow teenager was killed by a drunk driver. Kim's efforts at publicizing the issue were so successful that she was able to present a petition with 5,000 student signatures to the governor, who subsequently organized a state task force (on which Kim served) to combat the problem.

Over the past few years, a number of groups like Kim's have organized under the acronym SADD, which has stood variously for Students Against Drunk Driving, Students Against Drunk Drivers and Students Against Driving Drunk. The most well-known and largest (some 6,000 schools) of the SADD organizations is Students Against Driving Drunk, which was started in September 1981 by Robert Anastas, former director of health education for the Wayland Public School System in Wayland, Massachusetts. Mr. Anastas, a hockey coach who had lost two star athletes to drunk-driving accidents, makes presentations to high schools nationwide in which he tells students, "You have to find a solution."

The solutions SADD groups have devised have varied from community awareness programs and legal lobbying to "dry-high" parties (see the description of Project Graduation) and media campaigns. Every SADD group approaches its task differently, but almost all have a rally, or SADD Day at school, and all stress the SADD parent-teenager contract. Signed by both student and parent, the contract states that the student agrees to call home for help if he or she is ever too drunk to drive or would be forced to ride with a drunk friend. In return, the parent agrees to arrange safe transportation for the teen—no questions asked—and the parent also agrees to seek a safe ride if ever in similar circumstances.

"I know at least three kids who've used it," says David Haggerty, eighteen, who was president of the SADD chapter at West Genesee High School in Camillus, New York, until his graduation. "One hundred percent were glad. A friend of mine called his father after drinking too much, and his father came to pick him up. I was talking to him the next day, and I said, 'So, did you get killed?' He said, 'No, I think my father respected me almost more because I did use it.' Let's face it, we're all using our parents' cars, and secondly, it [drunk driving] is no joke."

In addition to encouraging fellow students to use the contract, David's group of about twenty core members organized an assembly. Preceding a presentation on drunk driving, the students put on a slide show that interspersed shots of school friends and teams with coroner's slides of accident victims. They also arranged for a wrecked vehicle to be placed in front of the school before prom night, and wrote and acted in two public service announcements illustrating drunk-driving situations. The group banded together originally in 1982, David notes, because of the impact of a speech given by a local student who had killed a forty-year-old husband and father in an accident after drinking a six-pack of beer. "He was telling us what the other kids think of you after you're a 'murderer,' as he called it, and how it affects your life," David says.

"When you get involved in SADD as a teenager, other kids may mock you out, but I think they're almost envious," David adds. "The same kids who came up to me last year and said, 'Oh, you're sad, Haggerty,' as a joke, were coming up to me this year and telling me what a good job I did."

It should be mentioned that some alcoholism professionals have expressed concern that SADD may have developed a conflict of interest by accepting funding from liquor industry groups such as the United States Brewers Association. There's no reason, however, why a student group can't raise its own funding to combat drunk driving.

Safe Rides

The Safe Rides system is another alternative to riding with a drunk driver. Although parents may be involved as advisers or drivers, the usual Safe Rides or "Dial-A-Ride" setup involves sober, trained teenagers with driver's licenses. They operate a confidential, on-call, nighttime ride service on high-risk occasions such as holidays, weekends, and prom night. The concept, which started in Darien, Connecticut, has since spread to school districts in such states as Maine, New York, New Hampshire, Maryland, and Wyoming.

"The best thing about Safe Rides is that it originated with and is directed by teenagers. Our motto is 'Youth serving youth,'" says Adam McManus, eighteen, who started a Safe Rides service at Westhill High School in Stamford, Connecticut.

To publicize the service, Adam initiated a survey to question students on their attitudes about drunk driving and to solicit volunteers. Fifty interested teenagers subsequently participated in an eight-hour program in which officials from the local alcoholism council and the Red Cross provided training in first aid and safety precautions. The group then obtained insurance as an Explorer Post, a program of the Boy Scouts of America. Although parents agreed to let their cars be used in this program, other Safe Ride services have obtained the cooperation of a local car dealer.

"The call comes in, and one person who's the dispatcher answers with 'Hi, Safe Rides, do you want a ride?'" Adam explains. "Then that person finds out all the necessary information. We always send out a boy and a girl together in a car, which is important—you can imagine what it would be like if one girl had to pick up two drunk guys. Each car is equipped with a large radio that plugs into the cigarette lighter, and has an antenna with a forty-mile radius. The people being picked up are asked to

91

wait outside. It's a very low-key thing," Adam stresses. "We don't arrive with loudspeakers telling everyone at the party, 'Here comes Safe Rides to pick up two idiots.'"

Headquartered in a church basement with an adult adviser present, the Stamford Safe Rides operates on Friday and Saturday nights year-round from 10 P.M. to 2 A.M. Through calling cards that advertise the service and emphasize that it's free and confidential, Adam was able to reach other teens right away: More than 500 used it in its first year and a half of service. About half, Adam says, were drunk or high themselves. The others were like Adam's first customers, two girls whose boyfriends had had too much to drink. The guys were staying overnight at their host's house and wanted their girlfriends to get home safely.

"We average about three or four calls a night," Adam says, "but I remember one night I drove eighty miles and picked up twenty-four drunk people. I hope some lives were saved."

The Control Factor

What's a *control factor*? According to this innovative Minnesota teen-to-teen program, it's a strategy—such as calling a Safe Rides service or hiding your friend's car keys—that combats the drunk-driving problem.

Developed by St. Cloud State University in 1981,

92

The Control Factor has spread to a number of states. The program consists of pairs of high school juniors and seniors conducting three-period classroom seminars for freshmen and sophomores on alcohol awareness and the hazards of drinking and driving. The teen instructors, who are recommended by their schools, are trained at one-day regional leadership workshops. In one recent year, 289 conducted programs for 5,828 of their peers.

Tools for The Control Factor include video segments on teenage substance abuse, drunk driving, and peer pressure; a question-and-answer game in which the class is divided into teams to test alcohol awareness; and worksheets on evaluating risks and consequences of drunk driving. In one session, for example, participants are asked to examine and judge the behavior of a number of fictional characters at a party where liquor is being served.

Pre- and post-program testing has shown that The Control Factor has a positive effect on teens' attitudes toward drinking and driving.

National Student Safety Program

The National Student Safety Program (NSSP) is open to any junior or senior high school student who wants to start a safety project or club. The program, sponsored by the American Driver Traffic Safety

93

Education Association, provides direct training only through a consultant service, but it does offer students free materials and guides to conducting programs in many areas of safety. On the subject of drunk driving, the NSSP has "The Price Is High," a skit with accompanying transparencies on alcohol myths and realities. Following a game-show format, the skit has participants play such roles as Miss Smart Aleck and Mr. Tell It Right. Also available is "Drinking and Driving: What Could You Do," a film about options. In addition, the NSSP publishes a newsletter, hosts a national conference, and distributes awards for outstanding school safety projects. The membership fee is $10 per school.

Project Graduation

The goal of Project Graduation is to keep prom and graduation festivities free of alcohol-related fatalities. It began in Maine in 1980 in response to a particularly tragic six-week pregraduation period in the state the preceding year: Twelve teenagers were killed in driving while intoxicated accidents (seven in one crash alone), and another was paralyzed.

To prevent a repeat of these statistics, a group of student and community leaders in the Oxford Hills area launched a massive campaign to host parties and activities that would celebrate graduation without chemicals. By 1983, Project Graduation had spread to eighty-six districts in Maine and other districts in more than twenty states nationwide. Although Project Graduation has the help of adult volunteers and police to keep away substance abusers and gate-crashers, its focus is parties so lavish and entertaining that students won't even *want* to attend a liquor-serving alternative party. Those festivities have included all-night riverboat cruises, dance marathons, barbecues with free films and celebrity appearances, and the renting of entire sports resorts with all courts open and bands playing until dawn. Although such galas are understandably expensive, the teens involved have been enormously successful not only in raising their own funds, but in getting donations of food and help from local businesses and free publicity from the media.

"We ran a free, chemical-free cruise the night of graduation," says Toby Seavey, nineteen, who was president of the 1984 class at Windham High School in Windham, Maine. "The students boarded a bus for Portland and then cruised Casco Bay until 6 the next morning. It provides an opportunity for the senior class to get together for the last time, and also it keeps them off the roads.

"We had meat and cheese platters, the Pepsi Cola bottler donated thirty cases of soda, and local merchants donated door prizes. We had a disc jockey on board with dancing, and upstairs we had cribbage and Monopoly games.

"In Maine, it's becoming more of a tradition to go

95

to a dry party or on a dry cruise after graduation, just like three or four years ago it was a tradition to go to someone's house and get 'blottoed.' "

Such efforts resulted in Maine seniors getting the best graduation present they have ever had in 1983: *no* alcohol-related teen fatalities in the entire state from May 15 to June 30.

All these projects try to prevent drunk-driving tragedies. But what of teenagers like Hector who have already suffered the consequences? Here are Hector's own words on his role in illustrating the problem to other teenagers, and his feelings about his future:

"When I started getting fan mail, then I knew something was happening. If kids were taking the time just to write to me, then I knew I had to affect some students. All I hoped for was that I would at least touch one student in every talk I gave. I know I am helping some people out there—I just know it.

"I don't worry about being paralyzed or being crippled for life. I've just got too much faith. . . . I've accepted it to be paralyzed for today, and that's it. Tomorrow, I might be walking. And if not, I'll just take that day and accept it. I'll just say again, 'Then I'll walk tomorrow' . . .

"I guess I've always had hope, but there were a few days when I broke down, just started crying. But I've really broken down very few times. Sometimes I just feel that I'm holding on to a string and somebody's on the other side saying, 'Follow me, and follow the way it's happening.' That's what keeps me going. I have a lot of faith that there's something out there that's stronger and something that can just click a finger and say, 'Here's your legs, and thank you for the beautiful job that you've done.'

"I believe that's the way it's going to happen."

CHAPTER SIX

Family Secret, Family Disease

"My father wasn't what I thought a father should be," says Kate. "I remember so many Christmases when he was passed out by 11 in the morning.

"At my college graduation, he was drunk. We were caught in this traffic jam on the main road. He started fighting with my mother, and then he got out of the car and started walking up the highway. This was my graduation, and I was crying. Every event that should have been happy wasn't—it was always marred by the drinking and the fighting and the embarrassment.

"My father flew out of the house one night because he said there were 'kooks lurking around the corner.' My mother had brought them in and he knew they were there. My sister was still in high school, and she and her boyfriend had to chase him, and they finally got the people from the hospital to come and get him. And when I came home weeks later, he took me to the window and pointed to the ocean and showed me where 'the big parade' had been marching on the water, and he told me one 'kook' had put his head through the doorknob and was really teasing him, and he'd punched one that was under the bed.

"It's funny—my sisters and I were never really frightened by this. My father would never physically hurt us. Basically, what we had was a feeling that we weren't loved, that he was more interested in drinking and passing out. It was more this disappointment that he wouldn't be there for us. I thought there must be something horribly wrong with me that my father was like that.

"When I see him drunk now, it's as if my heart has turned to stone."

Kate is one of an estimated 28 million Americans who are the children of alcoholics. Because she is an adult, the experience of growing up with a drinking parent is behind her. Nevertheless, Kate can't fully enjoy her personal and professional success. She still feels insecure and inadequate, convinced that she's going to "be found out, that everyone will know I'm just some drunk's daughter." And even though Kate has a home of her own, she confronts her father's drinking almost every family holiday.

Like alcoholism itself, being the child of an alcoholic affects the individual's entire life. Fortunately, the pain is treatable and is receiving more attention as health professionals become aware of the special problems facing children of alcoholics—young or old. Not only are they at increased risk of developing alcoholism themselves (see Chapter Two), but they are more likely to suffer from anxiety, depression, learning disabilities, and problems with peers than children of nonalcoholics. They are frequently the victims of violence and sexual abuse. They have higher suicide rates than the rest of the population. The daughters are also likely to marry alcoholics, making themselves even more the heirs to the family disease.

But although the statistics are frightening, not all children of alcoholics are battered or truant. Many, like Kate, feel only the emotional hurt. They may go on to become extremely high-achieving and responsible adults—so responsible that they find it difficult to relax and have fun. They may shun both alcohol and drinkers, but have other problems developing close relationships.

"I stayed single for a long time," says Kate, who is in her thirties. "I wondered, 'Do I keep picking men who don't like me, who can't make a commitment for life, or who are loners? I wonder what the alcoholism has done to me."

What alcoholism does to a family member depends on a variety of factors. Children who are already adolescents or young adults at the time the parent begins drinking feel the effects less severely than those who have to endure the parent's alcoholism from infancy. Some research contends that the most damaging alcoholism is that of the parent of the same sex as the child; other studies indicate that the mother's alcoholism, since she is likely to be the primary caretaker, has more devastating implications. Other factors are the stage of the parent's alcoholism and whether the other parent drinks, too—a not-uncommon situation that can overwhelm a child.

"My father used to drink very heavily—Scotch whiskey, Jack Daniels, Dewar's," recalls fifteen-year-old Jackie. "My mother was very suicidal, very hysterical, very violent. She was always drunk, and she used to hit my brothers and sisters a lot—and me.

"I was about ten when I knew what was going on. I realized that there were a lot of fights, and I started noticing my mother's drinking. The fights would always be about my father telling my mother that she drank too much. I think he was drunk too, but not quite as drunk as she was. My mother usually threw things at him, and he usually hit her, and one or both of them would leave the house."

Jackie sums up her reactions: "I was very upset; I was very suicidal. My grades were down the tubes, I didn't have any friends, I didn't want to bring anybody home. And I hated my parents."

Jackie's response was typical of a range of feelings these children experience.

Guilt

Many blame themselves for their parent's drinking. They feel that the only reason the family member doesn't exercise control is because he or she doesn't want to—doesn't love the child enough. They may also think that the parent uses drinking as a means to escape from or punish the child's bad behavior. Sometimes a mother or father will reinforce these emotions out of a desperate need to deny the disease.

"My mother got mad at something and started hitting me and slapping me around and kicking me," remembers Peggy, the thirteen-year-old daughter of alcoholics who are separated. "I tried everything to stay out of her way, which didn't work. Finally, she called up one of her friends and started blaming everything—I mean everything—on me. Like, 'I'm drinking because of my daughter. I don't want her, she's this and she's that . . .'

"In the beginning, I blamed myself. I would say, 'This is all my fault, I make her do this.' But at the same time, I'd be thinking, 'Well, it's her fault too, because if she wanted me with her, the least she could do is take care of me properly.'"

Resentment like Peggy's is another reason why children of alcoholics feel guilty. Many can't cope with the hostility their parents' actions arouse. And if an alcoholic parent is hurt in any way—a drunken fall, a car accident—the child may assume that he or she caused it by being angry.

"We've said someone should do our father a favor and push him off the pier," says Kate. "I cannot tell you how many times I've told him I hated him."

At the same time, Kate loves her father. Once, when she sought help from a psychologist about the problems in her family (both her uncles were also alcoholics), she came home from a therapy session and got a message that one of her uncles had died. Although this was only an unfortunate coincidence, Kate felt punished and failed to return for more treatment.

Fear

Kate's reaction was also typical of the fear a drinking parent provokes: fear that the parent will die behind the wheel or at home, fear that the parent will accidentally harm the rest of the family or abuse them in a drunken rage. In many instances, the fear is justified. Alcoholics do pass out in the driver's seat or on the couch with a cigarette in hand. Like Jackie's and Peggy's mothers, they may abuse their children.

Even children who aren't physically abused feel the fear that accompanies instability. The parent who was kind to them this morning may be critical and hostile this afternoon. The parent who, in a moment of sobriety, vowed to attend the class play may come drunk or not at all. The children live in a world of broken promises, a world whose basic elements can shift at any time: Parents divorce or can't take care of them, and they are shuttled back and forth between relatives or foster homes. Peggy's parents, for example, separated when she was a baby. At the age of six months, she was given to friends who took care of her for a year while her mother was drinking. Since then, she has lived sometimes with her mother, sometimes with family friends. She is now living with her father, who no longer drinks but feels no closeness to Peggy and has threatened to send her back to her mother if she doesn't take care of herself—a tall order when you're only thirteen.

Finally, a child may be afraid of approaching a nondrinking parent (if there is one). This parent maybe so absorbed in the spouse's illness that little time or patience remains for the child's problems.

"I never talked to anybody about anything," says Ted, who grew up with an alcoholic father and is now in his twenties. "There was one point when a gang of kids was chasing me around. I never told an adult because I was afraid I'd be blamed."

Shame

Claudia Black, a therapist who has worked extensively with children of alcoholics, has referred to an attitude like Ted's as "Don't talk, don't trust, don't feel." Children of alcoholics learn at an early age that they are not supposed to upset their parents and that it is wrong to bring up the drinking. The nondrinking parent may encourage this lack of communication in order to preserve an appearance of harmony. The nondrinker may have a misguided belief that the problem, if ignored, will go away, or at least won't be noticed by the children. Children, of course, do notice. Many report that at first they thought everybody's mother or father acted that way. Even when they know otherwise, later in life they frequently gravitate to relationships that repeat the same patterns.

"My parents were married twenty-three years," says Ted. "The two of them were nonconfrontational —not dealing with negative feelings. On rare occasions when anger erupted, it would be shattering to me. I grew up becoming what Al-Anon [a self-help organization for families of alcoholics] calls an *arrogant doormat*. To understand that, you have to live it. It comes from the insecurity of knowing your parents aren't there for you."

This insecurity often leads to isolation. Like Jackie, children of alcoholics may feel too ashamed to bring friends home, afraid that the drinking parent may behave in an embarrassing manner. Alcohol abuse becomes the family secret, sometimes so well-kept that the children become completely distanced from their own feelings about the problem. This is one reason why they may not seek available help.

"One day as we were driving to the beach, my mother explained this alcoholism thing to me," says Ted. "I was about eleven, and it didn't really scare me too much, because there was no relationship there to lose—it was like being told it about the next-door neighbor. She asked me later if I wanted to go to Alateen [a teen group affiliated with Al-Anon] and I said, 'No, I don't need that.' I was completely out of touch with my anger and my hurt.''

Researchers who have studied family dynamics note that close relatives adopt certain behaviors to minimize the confusion and pain of living with an alcoholic. In the researchers' analysis, the family is a system: a group of interdependent parts that act and react in order to attain stability, much as a mobile sways and moves in the force of the wind until its components achieve balance. In an alcoholic's family, the adaptation may be unhealthy for the individuals, but it enables them to stay together.

Some of those who have studied this phenomenon, including Claudia Black, have compared it to the adjustment process that takes place after a family is informed that one of its members has cancer. (Remember that alcoholism is also a disease.) The first stage is usually denial, with attempts to minimize or explain away the situation: "He is not really sick." What follows is often a kind of bargaining, in which children and others try to do things that they think will facilitate a magical cure. With alcoholism, this behavior may take the form of trying to please and accommodate the drinker to get the person to stop. Ironically, these actions may make it easier for the alcohol abuse to continue. The family (and sometimes friends and employers) will organize activities around the drinking rather than confront it as the problem.

"My father was one of the best-liked men in our

neighborhood," remembers Kate. "He would drink on his job. But, you see, an alcoholic is often the nicest guy in town. Everybody likes him—except his family."

As Kate points out, hostility usually accompanies the family's attempts to adjust. Conflicts arise with the nonalcoholic parent, too. Kate's father, for example, often blamed his drinking on his wife's nagging. Kate and her sisters came to resent their mother, even though she was no more responsible for the alcoholism than they were.

After so much turmoil, most families of alcoholics either dissolve or reach a state of acceptance. If the family stays together, the children will usually adopt roles that enable them to cope and the family to survive. Sharon Wegscheider, a clinician, writer, and chairperson of the San Francisco–based National Association for Children of Alcoholics, has identified these roles as follows:

The Family Hero

This child frequently substitutes for the incapacitated parent or parents by taking over household and parenting duties. Usually the oldest, the child compensates for the drinking problem by becoming an academic success and a high-achieving adult. Although this behavior may bring recognition, it doesn't raise the hero's self-esteem because the parental alcoholism remains.

"I was shy as a teen and maybe I knew doing well in school would be my ticket out," Kate says. She remembers, though, that her sisters resented her leaving for college because "I left the problem with them." Now that she has a whole list of achievements to her name, Kate still wonders, " 'Do I really deserve this?' "

Because heroes hold themselves to such rigid standards, they may find it hard to have fun, and drinking can become a temptation. Having taken on responsibilities for the entire family, they may feel unable to enter a relationship in which they're not in control. Most therapy for heroes focuses on helping them learn to express their feelings and to trust others.

The Scapegoat (or "Acting-out" or Problem Child)

The scapegoat (or "acting-out" or problem child) gets recognition in the opposite way from the hero. This child doesn't wish to make sacrifices to achieve self-worth. Instead, the child seeks support from a peer group, and acts out anger by being truant, getting into trouble, or abusing alcohol or drugs.

Jackie and Ted, for example, became scapegoat children. By the time Jackie was thirteen and entered AA, she was drinking a pint of liquor a day.

Ted remembers drinking heavily in high school. "It was the thing to do, it felt good, and it gave me this feeling that I was omnipotent," he says. Usually frightened and self-conscious around others, he turned to bizarre behavior to get attention.

"I'd act sad to get attention, I'd act crazy by running on top of cars," he remembers. "I'd make up lies and they'd backfire. This happened to me up until college—I had to have people be impressed by me."

Since scapegoat children so often turn to drugs and alcohol, they are at great risk of developing dependency. With treatment, they can learn to accept responsibility and to deal with their rage in less self-destructive ways.

The Lost Child

Claudia Black has also called these children *adjusters*. Whatever happens, they accept it. If there are family arguments, they will probably withdraw from the scene of conflict. If they have to move because of divorce, they will pack their bags without a complaint. Their coping mechanism is often to isolate themselves and retreat into a world of their own. Usually the younger children in the family, they appear very self-sufficient and adaptable. Inside, they usually feel lonely and powerless.

"They are the highest suicide risk," points out Dr. William C. Van Ost, founder and director of the Van Ost Institute for Family Living, a treatment center in Englewood, New Jersey, for families affected by chemical dependency. "They feel that no one knows they exist. If you talk to their high school teachers, they're the ones who never caused trouble in class."

If a lost child's lack of self-esteem goes untreated, alcohol may eventually be an attractive source of the omnipotent feelings Ted described.

The Family Mascot

The mascot or family pet thinks that the best way to minimize family tension is to provide comic relief. This child may appear charming and cute, while suffering from deep feelings of insecurity and inadequacy. Always good for a laugh, the child turns attention away from the pain of the drinking.

"As the oldest daughter of an alcoholic, I felt I had two roles," says an adult child of an alcoholic. "The first was that of hero—to bring fame and respectability to the family. My other role was to relieve the tension by being funny, and it wasn't until two or three years ago and after a lot of therapy that I broke the habit."

Another similar type of child—also warm, well-liked, and devoted to putting others at ease—is the placater. As defined by Claudia Black, the placater tries to smoothe over problems by offering sympathy and support. Like the mascot's jokes, the placater's constant sacrifices provide a sense of purpose and relief from guilt. Problems arise later, however, when the placaters find it impossible to attend to their own needs and wishes—or even to identify what

111

these are. They may marry alcoholics, who are emotional takers to whom they can give as selflessly as they gave to their parents. Alcohol may become their release from constant feelings of responsibility.

Whatever roles or combination of roles they adopt, children of alcoholics usually find it hard to go for help. If you have an alcoholic parent or family member, these points may help you come to terms with your feelings:

- *You are not responsible for the problem.* You can't control your parent's drinking, and neither can your parent; the disease is in control. And even though alcoholics can be treated, no one can force them to get help. Peggy remembers the time she flushed all her mother's pills (to which her mother was also addicted) down the toilet.

   "I said, 'I'm going to get you sober if it kills me,'" Peggy says. "She almost did kill me for it—literally. . . . Now I'm finally believing that alcoholism is a disease and not just drinking because you feel like it."
- *You are not alone.* An estimated 7 million people under twenty in the United States are children of alcoholics. Many well-known people have grown up in these circumstances: Actress and model Brooke Shields is the child of a recovered alcoholic, as is actor Steven Ford (son of former First Lady Betty Ford).

Actor Jason Robards and actress Kate Nelligan are from families affected by alcoholism. President Ronald Reagan has noted that his father had a drinking problem as well.

• *You have options.* Even though your parent has no choice about his or her behavior, you have control over yours. Make it a point to write a list of alternatives when you feel you may be trapped in an unpleasant situation. If, for example, you're afraid your father will be drunk when you bring friends home from school, your list might include seeing your friends away from home, inviting them over at a time when you know your father is sober, or explaining his illness to them and saying that you would prefer to spend your time outside. You can also confront your parents. Approach the drinker only when he or she is sober. You won't be able to change the behavior, but pointing out the ways in which the drinking hurts you may encourage your parent to get help. (See Intervention and Family Therapy later in this chapter.) You can also talk to your nondrinking parent. Explain that you are aware of the problem and that you would like your family to get help.

Peggy's behavior when her mother became drunk and violent was a good example of exercising a choice. Recovered alcoholics for whom Peggy baby-sat had told her that she could call them for help at any time. When

Peggy flushed the pills down the toilet and her mother began to abuse her, she left home and called these adult friends. They were able to pick her up and give her a place to stay.

- *You can trust other adults.* As Peggy realized, it's important to have older people to turn to in a crisis. They can be any adults you feel able to confide in: school counselors, teachers, your physician, a minister or rabbi, the parents of your friends. Doctors and mental health professionals are bound by their professional code of ethics not to divulge personal information from patients, so anything you say will remain confidential.

Keep in mind, too, that support groups throughout the country help children of alcoholics and many treatment programs deal with the entire family. The following are some important sources of help.

Alateen

Alateen is a special branch of Al-Anon, the national organization devoted to helping the families and friends of alcoholics. Alateen is similar to Al-Anon in that it employs the same principles of sharing and anonymity that were first established by Alcoholics Anonymous (see Chapter Seven); it is different in that its members are almost always adolescents.

Because Alateen serves the needs of a specific age group, it has its own standards. Teens wishing to form an Alateen group will need an adult participating member of Al-Anon to serve as a sponsor. This adult will guide the group in exploring problems relating to family alcoholism. Alateen also has Twelve Traditions, which are statements of purpose that serve as a guide to Alateen members. The traditions include unity, autonomy, self-support (there are no dues, only voluntary contributions) and the absence of any absolute authority but God. But while spiritual values are stressed in Alateen as they are in AA, the membership is nonsectarian. Teens from any religious or cultural background can and do belong.

What takes place at an Alateen meeting is relatively simple. The group gathers at an appointed time, usually once a week at a community center, schoolroom, or church hall. After one of the members reads an opening statement about Alateen, the group may decide on a theme for discussion. One Alateen group, for example, discussed the following statement at one of its meetings: "Sometimes I worry that I may become an alcoholic." Members of the group, who were sitting in a circle, one by one discussed their reactions to the statement and the extent to which they could identify with it. (No member, however, must offer comment; all participation is voluntary.) During the conversation, members were free to bring up related concerns. At the end of the meeting (most last about an hour and a half), the

115

group devoted several minutes to problem solving: Individual members brought up a recent problem relating to their experience as children of alcoholics. Other members then offered advice and support. The meeting concluded with a shared statement reaffirming the fellowship of Alateen.

While this meeting's format was typical, it is not universal. Other groups may be more or less structured. The purpose, however, is always the same: to come to a better understanding of the disease of alcoholism, and to encourage and support each other in coping with its effects.

"It's helped me a lot—not just with alcoholism, but with schoolwork," says Peggy about Alateen. "I like the slogans—like 'Let go and let God' and 'Live and let live.' The literature has helped me a lot because I feel I'm not the only one."

Intervention and Family Therapy

Intervention is a way of uniting the family members to get the alcoholic to admit the dependency and seek help. Interventions require a trained counselor and should not be performed without professional aid.

The first step in an intervention occurs when a family member contacts a treatment facility. The alcoholism counselor who will perform the intervention then brings together the important people in the alcoholic's life—children, siblings, parents, some-

116

times friends—and plans a caring confrontation with the alcoholic. The point is not to blame or wound the drinker, but to bring to the person's attention the consequences of the alcoholism in such a way that the issue can't be evaded. The family then asks the alcoholic to get help. Arrangements are made beforehand so that treatment can begin immediately if the alcoholic agrees. The family members must also be prepared with a list of alternative options of their own (for example, living apart from the drinker) if the alcoholic refuses treatment.

"The interventions we do consist of three nights of movies and lectures about alcoholism with family members and others who care about this person," says Elaine Van Ost of the Van Ost Institute for Family Living. "The fourth night is the dress rehearsal, during which they prepare exactly what they're going to say. The fifth night is the actual intervention, when the person is brought to our institute and faced with the results of his or her behavior. Often, this is the first time the person hears the truth. To do this, the family is encouraged to keep notes about the behavior, and then face the person with love. An example would be 'You came home drunk the other night and fell over the tea table,' and then you give your own feelings, such as 'I was very upset about that.' The idea is to present facts so that the alcoholic can't engage you in an argument. It's also said in a loving way, so that there's nothing to argue about."

Treatment for the alcoholic consists of therapy in a residential center. Many facilities maintain the bond with the family by including a family week at the end of the month or months of treatment or by holding sessions with family members (either separately or with the alcoholic) throughout the program. Family members are encouraged to join Al-Anon and/or Alateen to gain support and insight after the alcoholic's initial treatment (and theirs) is over. (For more on family therapy, see Chapter Seven.)

School Programs

Schools are becoming more involved in meeting the needs of children of alcoholics. Two programs that are currently being used as models across the country are the Student Assistance Program in Westchester County, New York, and the CASPAR program in Somerville, Massachusetts.

Although both programs have general alcohol-education components, they are also equipped to treat teenage children of drinkers separately. The Student Assistance Program, for example, is based on the Employee Assistance Programs that American businesses have used to identify and help chemical-dependent workers (and in some cases, their families). The children of alcoholics who can benefit from this counseling usually decide to come on their own, although they may be referred by teachers, relatives, or concerned friends. Except in instances where attendance is mandatory because a student was caught using alcohol or drugs, participation is voluntary and parental consent is not required. Meeting during their free periods, the teenagers gather in groups of five to ten for a minimum of eight sessions and a maximum of twenty. A trained social worker acts as the student assistance counselor, using group discussion to promote problem solving and enhance self-esteem. For further support, students are encouraged to join Alateen. If necessary, they may also see the counselor for individual help when the group sessions are over.

CASPAR (Cambridge and Somerville Program for Alcoholism Rehabilitation) uses peer counseling to help students understand the effects of family alcohol abuse. A pair of students who are themselves children of alcoholics are especially trained to lead the CASPAR CAF (Children from Alcoholic Families) groups, which meet confidentially after school.

Usually meeting one afternoon a week for ten sessions, the six to ten CAF participants learn about alcohol abuse through discussions, role-playing, journal-keeping, lectures, films, and field trips. All are paid $2 an hour to complete the course; leaders are paid $3.25 an hour. Participants are paid in order to encourage a wide attendance and avoid having embarrassment connected with the group. (For more information on these groups and other resources mentioned in this chapter, see the Appendix.)

It is important to remember that when you or your parent seek help, you may experience new problems that are part of the healing process. Even though sobriety is a positive change, it is still disruptive. You may have thought, for example, that your mother would be home every evening once she stopped drinking, and instead she is at AA meetings several times a week. You may resent her absence, and you may also resent being treated like a child again when you've been used to living life like an adult. Many children also feel enraged and despairing when their recovering alcoholic parent has a relapse. They need to be reassured that the episode doesn't mean that all hope is lost. They also need help in realizing that they still have a place in the family once the alcoholism is conquered. Some teenage children (and adults too) feel at a loss when they don't have to look after their parents or the younger children in the family any longer.

Support groups can be of enormous help in dealing with the recovery process as well as the disease. And even though recovery can be painful, children of alcoholics agree that the rewards are tremendous.

"Alateen showed me how to let go," says Jackie, whose mother has become sober through AA. "I can still love my mother, and I can let go of my father's drinking. I realize I can't make him stop, and I can't control his consumption, nor can I make him drink if I want to manipulate him. . . . I also don't get in fights so much with my mother. We're friends now, except that she has veto power over what I do."

CHAPTER SEVEN

Where To Go for Help

JIM DOESN'T REMEMBER many days from his drinking and drug involvement clearly, but he does recall the incident that spurred him to get help. He was seventeen, had recently quit school, and was descending into severe depression. One day, he decided to go to Boston to visit a friend who was in Alcoholics Anonymous. What happened to Jim after he got back meant more than anything his friend could tell him.

"The day I got home from Boston, I was sitting with a friend in a car, and I looked in my wallet and realized that I had lost all my money," Jim says. "I thought I was going crazy. I was really confused, and I started thinking about what had happened to it—did I spend it, was it the booze that I bought, the drugs that I bought? It sounds strange, but just that feeling of not knowing what I was doing made me realize that maybe it could be the drugs and the booze."

What happened to Jim is typical of the experiences

121

that bring teenagers into treatment. There might be an incident of illness or violence, an arrest or accident, or a confrontation with the family that makes them decide to get help. Sometimes, entry into treatment isn't voluntary: A teenager can be remanded by the courts or taken to a facility by parents. Frequently, both adult alcoholics and alcohol-abusing teens go for help when they recognize that their families will no longer put up with them, and that the pain of their drinking is outweighing the pleasure.

"My parents finally said, 'Hey, either you go into one of these drug rehabilitation centers and get help, or you can leave,'" recalls Alan, a nineteen-year-old from the Midwest who abused alcohol and other drugs from age nine until age sixteen. "So, automatically, I chose to leave."

But like many drinking teens, Alan found that life away from home was difficult and unsatisfying. After a week or two, he came back and agreed to his parents' demand. But even after he entered a hospital program, Alan had slipups. He left the program once and got drunk; his parents brought him back. He left a second time and returned to the hospital intoxicated. At that point, his doctors recommended that he go to an affiliated residential center for youth, where he was treated successfully. According to Alan, it wasn't so much the place that mattered, but his realization that there was no other source of hope.

"I was so hurt and so hopeless that I felt that it was

either this or it wasn't going to be anything at all," Alan says. "I was very suicidal. . . . I'd just had it with trouble. My parents had had it, my schools had had it, and the courts had had it. There were charges pending against me at the time—everything from assault and battery to being intoxicated under age."

As Alan points out, motivation is essential to a successful course of treatment. No professional organization, however, recommends waiting until a person hits rock bottom to seek help. The earlier a drinker gets treatment, the greater the chances are of arresting dependency and preventing long-term physical and psychological damage. That means facing the problem when the warning signs first appear.

"I looked back on things and saw they were getting worse," remembers twenty-year-old Beth. "Like not remembering what happened, and waking up and having my whole day ruined. It feels like you have the flu when you're really hung over, and here I was doing it to myself on purpose—everything seemed so self-destructive. Looking at it, I figured out that drinking was my main problem."

Getting Help

When a teenager wants help, many choices are available. But despite the differences in setting and length of treatment time, most adolescent programs have the following points in common.

Focus on the substance abuse itself

Although all reputable programs deal with the abuser's feelings and background, the immediate goal is always to get off the chemical. Teenagers are encouraged to replace alcohol and drugs with alternative highs—creative projects, athletics, academic achievement, friendships. In a substance-free environment, other teens provide the necessary support and understanding. Responsible behavior is rewarded by the facility's staff with increased privileges; failure to play by the rules is punished with the withdrawal of the same.

Emphasis on structure

Most programs for teenagers are highly structured. One reason is practical: There is lost time to make up. Courses are necessary to teach the academic, social, and job skills that teen abusers missed when they were high. Other reasons are therapeutic. Both adult alcoholics and their teenage counterparts frequently have lives that lack structure. Having to make the bed, cook meals, hold down a job in the facility, and perform other tasks are steps to a productive existence. Performing work successfully also enhances self-esteem. Finally, strict schedules prevent boredom, one of the biggest enemies of sobriety.

Rules are also important because they preserve the integrity of the therapeutic community. Although they vary from program to program and with the stage of treatment, these are basic to most:

124

- Absolutely no use of alcohol or drugs during treatment.
- No violent behavior.
- No dating or sexual activity between participants.

Although some teenagers resent the rules when they enter treatment, most, like sixteen-year-old Rebecca, change their minds.

"I hated it at first, because when I came into Daytop, I wasn't allowed to see my boyfriend or any of my friends for a month," says Rebecca, who was treated at one of the program's nonresidential, outreach centers. "I'd sit and cry every day because I couldn't see him. The others would say, 'Well, he's not good for you anyway,' and I'd say, 'Oh, you don't know him.' But it wound up that he really wasn't. They made me realize that he was running me down."

Use of group dynamics

Group therapy is an important facet of almost all programs for teenagers. Participants meet in small groups, always under the leadership of a counselor or therapist, to discuss their emotions, problems, and ways of dealing with each other. This approach includes resolving hostile or insecure feelings by talking them out rather than resorting to alcohol or some other substance. The group is also a forum in which the abuser can't exercise denial. Because peers are constantly observing and confronting the abuser on issues related to drinking or drugs, he or she can't pretend the problem doesn't exist. Support for staying sober is also being provided. Whereas friends from the old crowd participated in the abuse and encouraged it, this group is saying that happiness lies in not drinking and not taking drugs.

"The feedback from my peers helped me a lot," says Jim, who was treated for substance abuse at both a private psychiatric hospital and at Brattleboro Retreat, a Vermont residential facility for adolescents. "And when you're helping someone else out, you're also helping yourself grow. Say, for example, I was a patient and I'd been in two and a half months, and then a new person comes in. I'm pretty comfortable with what's going on, so I can help them out, and then they do well."

Family therapy

Another group that plays an important part in any alcohol abuser's recovery is the family. More and more treatment programs are now involving not only parents, but brothers and sisters. The family members may meet with the therapist without the person in treatment, or they may all meet together. Some programs include both options, as well as an opportunity for families to meet with other families.

Because alcoholism is considered a family disease (see Chapter Six), the treatment focuses on how the abuse has affected the family's functioning, and how its members can give support to the recovering person and also attend to their own needs. (Frequently, the problem of substance abuse supersedes all other concerns.) The family members can become aware of how they may have enabled the abuse to continue by refusing to confront the problem or by covering it up. In turn, the teenager in treatment can talk with parents and siblings about some of the more uncomfortable feelings—guilt and anger—that may have arisen in conjunction with drinking or drugs.

"We had family therapy once a week," says Jim, who was exposed to the process at both facilities. "There were a lot of tears and frustration, but it was good that those feelings were brought up. My mother and I did most of the talking. I think my mother had begun to accept the fact that I had a problem, but my father was still denying it."

With the help of two therapists who sat in on the sessions, Jim's family achieved a new understanding. "I think we've become a lot closer because of what I've been through," he says. "We've learned how to depend upon each other and trust each other."

Emphasis on the principles of AA

Although AA is a treatment unto itself (see pages 133-39), its principles are an important component for almost all other therapies. AA, which is a self-help organization for alcoholics, employs all the elements of group therapy already discussed. Members meet—anonymously—in easily accessible locations such as community centers or church basements to share feelings about drinking and to give each other support. The goal of an AA member is sobriety, or complete abstinence from alcohol. The AA route to sobriety is through the "twelve steps" (see pages 137-38). Although not every center may emphasize all aspects of AA, the AA focus on admitting the problem and the hurts it has caused, plus taking direct responsibility for sobriety, are in line with most treatments. Because AA is available to anyone, anywhere (it has chapters all over the world), most treatment centers encourage recovering alcoholics to become familiar with and involved in its program to help themselves maintain sobriety.

"In AA, the whole idea of the program is people helping each other," says Jim. "That's how I stay straight—by helping other people who have the same problem."

If these are the similarities in treatment for teenagers, what are the differences? Here are the sources of help:

Residential Treatment Centers

Residential treatment centers are best for teenagers who have a severe drinking or substance-abuse problem. Those who have been unable to continue with school or work because of alcohol or drugs have the greatest chance of success in a controlled environment.

Most facilities have a program that incorporates academics and athletics, as would any school. Teens can often finish high school while being treated. And whereas some have strict limits at first, many allow recovering teens to have weekend passes and make small trips away from the center after progress has been made.

How can you find a good program? The list of organizations in the Appendix is an important resource. In addition, your state's division on alcohol and drug abuse (look it up in the Yellow Pages) can provide leads, as can the local branch of the American Medical Association and your family physician. Major hospitals in large metropolitan areas or hospitals affiliated with medical schools frequently have alcohol and substance abuse programs of their own. Although these are usually short (six to eight weeks) and may not be geared specifically to adolescents, they incorporate the same principles of group and family therapy, plus aftercare visits on an outpatient basis that can continue for several months or a year or more. Once you hear of a program, you should be able to visit it with your family to see how it operates.

Before a teenager enters a residential program, an *intake* process includes a thorough physical examination by a physician and a psychological evaluation. These determine the extent of the problem and the individual's needs. Teenagers whose drinking or drug abuse is connected with mental illness or a major psychiatric disorder would probably be referred to a hospital devoted to those problems rather than to a residential center that focuses mainly on the abuse.

129

Similarly, someone who is so addicted that severe physical withdrawal symptoms would result might need to be hospitalized for *detoxification* before entering a residential program with other teens.

What is life like at a residential center? Here is how Kathy describes a day at Daytop Village:

"You wake up at 7, and you make your bed and clean your room. Then you have a morning meeting with the whole 'family' and you discuss what happened the day before—who may have been acting out, and how to help. There's usually a theme to it. It's also for you to gain confidence and learn to talk in front of others. There are also seminars in the evening for this, like ones on current events.

"During the day, you have a job. You may be on the kitchen team for cooking when you first come in. It's easy to do. A little later, you'll get more responsibility, and you have a boss like in a regular job. You might be a switchboard operator or work with the files.

"I took typing and shorthand, and since I got my equivalency here, I can take vocational courses. After school, there's exercise class—you might swim or play baseball. After dinner, there's free time for two hours.

"You come back downstairs at 7:30 for groups. There are groups Monday, Wednesday, and Friday. Newer residents have groups every day. You can go to your group leader during the week and talk if you have to. The staff is very generous with time."

130

Some treatment programs operate in stages. Daytop, for example, has phases of reentry. After a year to a year and a half in residence, participants go to another center where they live while they go to either school or work. Residents cannot graduate from the program until they have saved money and located an apartment.

Parkside Lodge, a youth center in the Chicago area affiliated with Lutheran General Medical Center, has a shorter program, incorporating four to six weeks of residential treatment. After treatment is completed, young people have the option of living at Parkside Youth Center, a halfway house where they can continue therapy while working or going to school. Both Beth and Alan chose the halfway house after treatment at Parkside.

"We'd get up and go to school or work, then come back and there would be a group meeting, a small group discussion, and then at night, an AA meeting," Alan says. He notes that the others' presence helped him stay sober. "I'd talk to someone about it instead of going out and getting drunk," he says. "Before, I'd just go out and do it."

How much does treatment at a residential center cost? Usually, there are options for every income level. Many parents' employee insurance programs cover some form of alcohol abuse treatment, including help for family members. And whereas private hospitals may charge $200 a day or more for a six-week program, public facilities may charge no fees at all. Organizations like Daytop, which is partially

131

state-supported and partially funded through private contributions, may also operate free of charge.

Outpatient Treatment

Outpatient treatment can be very successful for teenagers whose problems seem not to require the intensive, twenty-four-hour environment of a residential facility. For example, the evaluating therapists might decide that a teenager living at home with parents and still attending school should remain with the family while undergoing treatment. If difficulties arise in an outpatient setting, the teenager might be referred to a residential center. Frequently, teens assist in the decision. Jim, for example, realized that he was not benefiting from the sessions with his psychologist—a form of outpatient therapy—and elected, with his parents, to seek help from a private hospital and from Brattleboro Retreat.

Teens who enter outpatient programs specifically geared to young substance abusers will often find that treatment principles are similar to those at residential facilities.

Daytop Village's outreach program, for example, operates six days a week. The teenagers involved come to the center for therapy sessions, group activities, and school lessons from 9 A.M. to 5 P.M. On Saturday, they come in to clean the facility and for recreation from 10 A.M. until 3 P.M.

This program also has phases. After six or eight

132

months in Phase I, the teenagers go back to school or work while continuing in group and individual therapy in the evening. If teenagers come to Daytop with a drinking problem that is in an early stage, they may require only the afterschool/evening care part of the program. Many other facilities in the United States operate on a similar basis, offering structure according to the individual's needs.

Sandy was treated at one of Daytop's outreach centers. She found that she didn't need to be in a residential center to make the commitment to stop drinking.

"I figured if I'm going to come in here and get the help, I might as well stop," she says. "Plus, I was afraid of getting in trouble. If I kept on getting high or drinking, they'd have to tell my parents. And I didn't want to face the guilt that I'd feel. I felt that it was something wrong.

"Now that I'm back in school, my grades have flown up. I haven't gotten anything below ninety-eight so far. I'm more interested in school, and I'm taking computers on my own—in my old school, I didn't care about class. I can be trusted and I'm honest. I haven't taken one drink in almost a year now."

Alcoholics Anonymous

The scene is a community center basement. A group of about a dozen people—some teenagers, some middle-aged—are sitting around a table. After

133

a few minutes of coffee and conversation, an attractive young woman stands up to address the group.

"Hi," she says. "My name is Andrea and I'm an alcoholic and a drug addict. I'm the first daughter in my family and I was supposed to grow up and be somebody special. But I felt I wasn't pretty enough, I wasn't smart enough, I wasn't anything enough. Being high was a way to escape all those feelings. I was very scared of growing up and I hated change. . . .

"I drank to the point of a blackout my first time drinking. I ended up getting busted and I peed in a hallway. At a real young age, I was a sneak. I was always throwing up, being given coffee and walked around—and that was my social drinking. I also took downers. I'd be stoned before the party was even thought of. . . .

"I became a junkie, and told everyone except those in authority. I got thrown out of high school and boarding school. I decided, 'Oh, my problem is high school, my family, all the nuns.' . . .

"I knew I was lying to myself. . . . I was sick and really suicidal. Toward the end, my bottom was that there weren't enough drugs and alcohol to take away my pain anymore. . . . But I never thought there'd be a way for me to stay straight.

"I loved AA from the first day I got here. I knew I could do it—I kept coming back. They told me total abstinence was the only way for me and I bought it. My own ideas had never got me straight, so I just listened. . . ."

134

After Andrea's speech, a number of those sitting around the table comment. One young woman remembers that she was always trying to "be everything" and that alcohol became a way to cope with the anxiety. A young man recalls that he was "an emotional desert" and that for years he hadn't cried because the drinking blocked it out. More members of the group talk about why they drank and why they're sober now. At the end of the meeting, the members join hands and say a prayer together. Their leader reminds them, "Don't drink, and go to meetings."

What has taken place here is typical of AA. Someone like Andrea, who has been sober for several years, may give a speech to the group to stimulate discussion. Her way of referring to herself —by first name only, followed by "and I'm an alcoholic"—is what you'll hear at such meetings everywhere. First names are used to preserve anonymity. "I'm an alcoholic" is an expression of the AA belief that once you're dependent on drinking, you remain so for life. You can achieve sobriety, but you will always be an alcoholic.

How does AA work? As someone will point out at virtually every meeting, there are no dues or fees for membership—the only requirement is a desire to stop drinking. If you have that desire, no one will attempt to analyze whether or not you are clinically alcoholic. If you believe you need AA, that is sufficient. Anyone can join simply by coming to a meeting. Lists of meetings are published by the AA affiliate in your area. (Look in the Yellow Pages, or write to the address in the Appendix.) All information in AA groups is kept confidential.

Someone who joins AA may find it helpful to have a sponsor. A sponsor is another AA member who agrees to help the newcomer by accompanying him or her to meetings and by being an on-call resource in times of trouble. A member who feels resolve waning and is tempted to have a drink can call the sponsor instead.

The object of AA is to achieve sobriety. In AA, you make the commitment not to drink on a daily basis; you don't promise for a year, but for today. "One day at a time" and "easy does it" are popular AA slogans. Each day you successfully carry out that commitment is a worthy anniversary, whether it's your third day without alcohol or your third year. The goal in each case, however, is total abstinence. AA does not believe alcoholics can ever go back to drinking socially.

Although AA encourages spiritual faith as an aid to sobriety, it is not necessary to be religious or to belong to any faith to be a member. AA is not affiliated with any church or group. The focus is on self-help—for alcoholics to help themselves and each other by sharing feelings about drinking and by giving each other support.

The central philosophy of AA is expressed in the Twelve Steps.

Twelve Steps of Alcoholics Anonymous*

1. We admitted we were powerless over alcohol—that our lives had become unmanageable.
2. Came to believe that a Power greater than ourselves could restore us to sanity.
3. Made a decision to turn our will and our lives over to the care of God *as we understood Him.*
4. Made a searching and fearless moral inventory of ourselves.
5. Admitted to God, to ourselves and to another human being the exact nature of our wrongs.
6. Were entirely ready to have God remove all these defects of character.
7. Humbly asked Him to remove our shortcomings.
8. Made a list of all persons we had harmed, and became willing to make amends to them all.
9. Made direct amends to such people wherever possible, except when to do so would injure them or others.
10. Continued to take personal inventory and when we were wrong, promptly admitted it.

---

*The Twelve Steps reprinted with permission of Alcoholics Anonymous World Services, Inc., copyright 1939, 1952, 1976.

11. Sought through prayer and meditation to improve our conscious contact with God, *as we understood Him,* praying only for knowledge of His will for us and the power to carry that out.
12. Having had a spiritual awakening as the result of these steps, we tried to carry this message to alcoholics, and to practice these principles in all our affairs.

What help does AA offer to teenagers?

"I go to a minimum of three meetings a week," says Alan. "That's the most important thing for me—without it, I couldn't stay sober. I feel that the steps are most important and that these are the tools that give me a way of life to live—with them, I can feel happy and not get drunk."

But although AA is an important component of aftercare, more and more young people are using it as a primary resource. Anxious to extend "the hand of AA" to teens as well as adults, many AA chapters are establishing special young people's groups for members in their teens and twenties. Teens who are interested in finding out more about AA can also take advantage of open meetings that any concerned individual can attend, whether or not that individual has a drinking problem.

AA's triennial surveys of membership also show that more youths are participating. Its 1983 random survey of 7,611 AA members indicated that

20 percent of the group is under thirty—a 5 percent increase from the 1980 survey.

Jackie is one teenager who gained sobriety completely through AA. She found that she identified with the feelings expressed at the meetings, even though she was younger than anyone she'd ever met through the fellowship.

"If you find yourself going to AA meetings, there's no such thing as a high or low bottom," she points out. "You go through all the pain you have to go through to get there, or else you wouldn't be there. If you find yourself at AA meetings saying to yourself, 'Well, I don't think I'm an alcoholic,' remember that people don't go there because they're wondering. If it looks like a duck, walks like a duck, and acts like a duck, it's a duck."

Peer to Peer Counseling

Peer to peer counseling is not really treatment, but a form of early intervention. A number of programs across the country are now training teens to perform this service, either in school districts or at the state level. Whereas some programs, such as CASPAR (see Chapter Six), provide teens with the resources to set up discussion groups and refer their peers for further help, others focus more on combating drunk driving (see Chapter Five) or on educating teens to the realities of alcohol. PREP (Peer Resource Education Program), for example, was established by the Ozaukee Council on Alcohol and Other Drug Abuse in Port Washington, Wisconsin. Through the program, six teens from each county school district are trained each year to deliver alcohol awareness presentations to fifth and eighth graders, who are considered to be at critical ages. The teen instructors employ films and discussion to teach their younger classmates about chemical dependency, how to say no, and alternatives to abuse.

How are teens trained to be helpers? Usually, resources within the county or state sponsor training sessions that range from weekend retreats with monthly follow-up meetings to workshops that span several days. A number of states, including Ohio, Illinois, Missouri, and Wisconsin, sponsor teen institutes each year. During these programs, selected teens participate in training sessions for a few days to a week or more, usually during the summer. Those who apply and are accepted (often on the basis of leadership qualities and commitment to community work) are exposed to broad-based programs that deal with everything from learning about alcoholism and planning prevention projects to increasing students' self-awareness. Institute fees, which vary, are frequently paid through scholarships provided by local organizations and businesses.

"We start working with the kids to develop their own uniqueness and esteem, and they go back to their schools to start up programs," points out Robert L. Steele, coordinator of Ohio's Teenage Institute for the Prevention of Alcohol and Other Drug Abuse.

Most institutes lead not only to prevention activities in the participants' schools, but to the growth of other teen organizations and "mini-institutes" throughout the state. Operation Snowball, for example, grew out of the Illinois Teenage Institute on Substance Abuse (ITI). A number of teens who graduated from that program in 1977 set up youth groups throughout the state. Those Snowball support groups are now active in fund raising, sponsoring alcohol awareness workshops, speaking to other teens about peer resources, and setting up scholarships to ITI.

What does it feel like to be part of a youth prevention program? Toby Seavey, who participated in the Alcohol, Other Drug and Highway Safety Team Development Institute in Maine, discovered that he was able to implement what he had learned in a series of activities in his school.

"We had a two-day workshop where we took students out of the high school by grade and spent the time educating them about alcohol and drug abuse," Toby says. "We held two awareness sessions the first year. The second year, we did one for ninth grade students and a short presentation with that year's seniors to remind them of the hazards of drinking and driving around graduation. The third year, we also held an awareness session for sixth and

141

seventh grades. For the high school age group, we used films like 'I'll Quit Tomorrow' and 'Soft Is the Heart of a Child.' For sixth and seventh grades, we had a half-day workshop with one movie, two lectures, and a small group for discussion."

If you're interested in initiating prevention activities in your area, contact the state agency that handles substance abuse—this could be the state council on alcoholism, state department of health or mental health, or a special bureau on substance abuse. Programs may be already available to help interested teens.

Is Abstinence Necessary?

Whether teenagers are investigating treatment or being trained in prevention, one of the issues that will arise is the importance of abstinence for alcohol abusers. Anna once believed that she could go back to social drinking.

"I even celebrated a one-year anniversary with AA," she remembers. "I went back to work, and I threw a shower for a girl I worked with. Later on in the day, I found out that the punch a friend had made for the party—and that I'd drunk—had had some liquor in it. When I got home, I thought, 'My God, my world didn't fall apart the way they said it would in AA.' A month or so later, I was out to dinner and someone sent over an after-dinner cordial to my table. I had that, and again my world didn't fall apart. A week passed, and I had one more—I was testing it. All of a sudden, I started to buy alcohol again—I thought, 'Why not have a bottle in the house?' Within six months to a year, I was really messed up again."

What happened to Anna is very common. Whereas a little alcohol may seem to do no harm, it is extremely rare for the recovered alcoholic—whose drinking was previously out of control—to be able to contain consumption.

What does this mean for teenagers, who may abuse alcohol but not be chemically addicted? Because of the risk of developing adult alcoholism, most teenagers who have been through treatment find that they don't wish to drink at all. Alan, like many other recovered teens, feels that he is happier now than he ever was as a drinker.

"The way I talk, walk, dress, my appearance—it's all different," Alan says. "My goals and my attitudes have changed. I'm now capable of holding a job. I graduated from high school, and there was no way I could have done that before. I made the honor roll for one year, and that had never happened before.

"Really," he says, "the only thing about me that's the same now as before is my name. Anything else is just coincidental."

Appendix

Organizations dispensing alcohol abuse and prevention information and/or treatment referrals nationwide:

Alcoholics Anonymous World Services, Inc.
P.O. Box 459
Grand Central Station
New York, New York 10163

American Council on Alcohol Problems
2908 Patricia Drive
Des Moines, Iowa 50322

Johnson Institute
510 First Avenue North
Minneapolis, Minnesota 55403

National Black Alcoholism Council
417 South Dearborn Street
Chicago, Illinois 60605

National Clearinghouse for Alcohol Information
Box 2345
Rockville, Maryland 20852

National Council on Alcoholism, Inc.
12 West 21st Street
New York, New York 10010

National Institute on Alcohol Abuse and
Alcoholism
National Institute on Drug Abuse
5600 Fishers Lane
Rockville, Maryland 20857

National PTA Drug and Alcohol Abuse Prevention Project
National PTA
700 Rush Street
Chicago, Illinois 60611–2571

Women for Sobriety, Inc.
P.O. Box 618
Quakertown, Pennsylvania 18951

Resources for Children of Alcoholics

Alateen and Al-Anon
Al-Anon Family Group Headquarters
P.O. Box 182
Madison Square Station
New York, New York 10159–0182
Free booklet: "Facts About Alateen"

Children of Alcoholics Foundation, Inc.
540 Madison Avenue
New York, New York 10022

National Association for Children of
Alcoholics
P.O. Box 421691
San Francisco, California 94142

Organizations Combating Drunk Driving

The Control Factor
John W. Palmer, Coordinator
Youth Overinvolvement Project

APPENDIX

St. Cloud State University
Center for Driver Education and Safety
St. Cloud, Minnesota 56301

National Student Safety Program
Robert Ulrich
Humphreys 213
Safety Department
Central Missouri State University
Warrensburg, Missouri 64093

Project Graduation
c/o Margaret Thayer
Alcohol, Other Drugs and Highway Safety
Consultant
Division of Alcohol and Drug Education Services
Stevens School Complex
State House Station #57
Augusta, Maine 04333
Free booklet: "Project Graduation: Friends for Life"

Remove Intoxicated Drivers (RID)
P.O. Box 520
Schenectady, New York 12301

Safe Rides
c/o First United Methodist Church
Cross Road
Stamford, Connecticut 06905

Students Against Driving Drunk (SADD)
110 Pleasant Street
Corbin Plaza
Marlboro, Massachusetts 01752

For more information on how drinking can affect you, write for the following pamplets:

- "Will You Make It Home Tonight?" can be obtained by sending a stamped, selfaddressed business-sized envelope to the National Safety Council, Department PR, 444 North Michigan Avenue, Chicago, Illinois 60611.

147

- "One Drink Can Be Too Many" is available free or at nominal charge from your local Automobile Association of America club. (Look for the listing in the white pages of the phone book.)

Treatment and Prevention Programs Mentioned in This Book

Brattleboro Retreat
75 Linden Street
Brattleboro, Vermont 05301

CASPAR
226 Highland Avenue
Somerville, Massachusetts 02143

Daytop Village, Inc.
54 West 40th Street
New York, New York 10018

Ohio Teen Institute
Robert L. Steele, Coordinator
Ohio Department of Health
Teenage Institute for the Prevention of Alcohol and Other Drug Abuse
Bureau on Alcoholism
P.O. Box 118
Columbus, Ohio 43216

Operation Snowball
Illinois Alcoholism and Drug Dependence Association
401 West Highland Avenue
Springfield, Illinois 62704

Parkside Lodge
24647 North Highway 21
Mundelein, Illinois 60060

Peer Resource Education Program (PREP)
Ozaukee Council on Alcohol and Other Drug Abuse
125 North Franklin Street
Port Washington, Wisconsin 53074

148

APPENDIX

Student Assistance Program
Ellen Morehouse
Program Director
School-Based Programs
Westchester County Department of Community Mental Health
112 East Post Road
White Plains, New York 10601

Van Ost Institute for Family Living, Inc.
113 Engle Street
Englewood, New Jersey 07631

Programs in Canada

Addiction Research Foundation
33 Russell Street
Toronto, Ontario M5S 2S1

Alcoholism and Drug Dependence Commission of New Brunswick
43 Brunswick Street
P.O. Box 6000
Fredericton, New Brunswick E3B 5H1

Nova Scotia Commission on Drug Dependency
5675 Spring Garden Road
Halifax, Nova Scotia B3J 1H1

Alcohol and Drug Program
P.O. Box 1320
Yellowknife, Northwest Territories X1A 2L9

Alcoholism Foundation of Manitoba
1031 Portage Avenue
Winnipeg, Manitoba R3G 0R9

Saskatchewan Alcohol and Drug Abuse Commission
3475 Albert Street
Regina, Saskatchewan S4S 6X6

Alberta Alcohol and Drug Abuse Commission
10909 Jasper Avenue, 7th Floor
Edmonton, Alberta T5J 3M9

Alcohol and Drug Dependency Commission of
Newfoundland
6 Logy Bay Road
St. John's, Newfoundland A1A 1J3

Bibliography

Black, Claudia. "Innocent Bystanders at Risk: The Children of Alcoholics." *Alcoholism/The National Magazine,* January–February 1981.

——. *It Will Never Happen to Me!* Denver: MAC, 1981.

Blakeslee, Sandra. "Scientists Find Key Biological Causes for Alcoholism." *The New York Times,* August 14, 1984.

Capuzzi, Dave, and Lecoq, Lindy Low. "Social and Personal Determinants of Adolescent Use and Abuse of Alcohol and Marijuana." *The Personnel and Guidance Journal,* December 1983.

Christiansen, Bruce A., and Goldman, Mark S. "Alcohol-Related Expectancies Versus Demographic Background Variables in the Prediction of Adolescent Drinking." *Journal of Consulting and Clinical Psychology,* Vol. 51, No. 2, 1983.

Collins, Glenn. "Alcoholism: Treating the Family as a Whole." *The New York Times,* December 8, 1982.

——. "One Family's Experiences With Alcoholism Therapy." *The New York Times,* December 9, 1982.

Donovan, John E., Jessor, Richard, and Jessor, Lee. "Problem Drinking in Adolescence and Young Adulthood: A Follow-up Study." *Journal of Studies on Alcohol,* Vol. 44, No. 1, 1983.

ARE YOU DYING FOR A DRINK?

Golden, Sandy. *Driving the Drunk Off the Road: A Handbook for Action.* Washington, D.C.: Acropolis Books, 1983.

Goldman, Mark S. "Cognitive Impairment in Chronic Alcoholics: Some Cause for Optimism." *American Psychologist,* October 1983.

Graeber, Laurel. "Hitting Rock Bottom: The Compelling Story of a Young Woman's Battle with Alcoholism." *Young Miss,* August, 1983.

Heil, Andrea. "Drunk Driving: Everybody Loses." *Young Miss,* November 1983.

Hennecke, Lynn, and Gitlow, Stanley E. "Alcohol Use and Alcoholism in Adolescence." *New York State Journal of Medicine,* June 1983.

Konigsberg, David, Weinhouse, Beth, and Wechsler, Joan. "Teenagers and Alcohol: Holiday Hazard, Year-round Tragedy." *Ladies' Home Journal,* December 1983.

Lieber, Charles S. "The Metabolism of Alcohol." *Scientific American,* March 1976.

Little, Ruth E. "Drinking During Pregnancy: Implications for Public Health." *Alcohol Health and Research World,* Fall 1979.

Marlatt, G. Alan, and Rohsenow, Damaris J. "The Think-Drink Effect." *Psychology Today,* December 1981.

National Institute on Alcohol Abuse and Alcoholism. "Facts for Planning: Alcohol and Youth." Selected reprints from *Alcohol Health and Research World,* Fall 1982–Spring 1983.

———. "A Growing Concern: How To Provide Services for Children From Alcoholic Families." Washington, D.C.: U.S. Department of Health and Human Services, 1983.

———. "The Secretary's Conference for Youth on Drinking and Driving." Washington, D.C.: U.S. Department of Health and Human Services, 1983.

BIBLIOGRAPHY

————. "Treatment Services for Youth." (Reprint from *Alcohol Health and Research World,* Summer 1983.) Washington, D.C.: U.S. Department of Health and Human Services, 1983.

————. "Youth and Alcohol: Prevention at the State Level." (Reprint from *Alcohol Health and Research World,* Fall 1981.) Washington, D.C.: U.S. Department of Health and Human Services, 1981.

Segal, Bernard. "Drugs and Youth: A Review of the Problem." *The International Journal of the Addictions,* Vol. 18, No. 3, 1983.

Schneider, Max A. "Alcohol and Nutrition." Santa Ana, Calif.: Max A. Schneider, M.D., Inc., 1982.

————. "Some Medical Aspects of Alcohol and Other Drugs of Abuse." Santa Ana, Calif.: Max A. Schneider, M.D., Inc., 1982.

Vaillant, George E. *The Natural History of Alcoholism.* Cambridge, Mass.: Harvard University Press, 1983.

Wegscheider, Sharon. "From the Family Trap to Family Freedom." *Alcoholism/The National Magazine,* January–February 1981.

Woodside, Migs. "Children of Alcoholics." Albany, N.Y.: New York State Division of Alcoholism and Alcohol Abuse, July 1982.

153

Index

Abstinence, 142–43
Acetaldehyde, 34, 36
Acute alcoholic hepatitis, 61
Acute alcohol poisoning, 51, 52–53
Adjusters, 110–11
Adolescent programs, 123–43
  AA, 133–39
  outpatient treatment, 132–33
  peer to peer counseling, 139–42
  points in common, 123–28
  residential treatment center,
    128–32
  sources of help, 128–43
Aggression, 43
Al-Anon, 106, 114, 118
Alateen (AA-affiliated group), 24,
  106, 114–16, 118
Alcohol, Other Drug and Highway
  Safety Team Development
  Institute (Maine), 141
Alcohol-dependent, 15
Alcoholic cardiomyopathy, 62
Alcoholic hepatitis, 60
Alcoholic personality, 31
Alcoholics, 27–37
  cultural group, 32–34
  in the family, 35–37
  misconceptions about, 30
  mortality rate, 14, 83
  myths, 31–32
  See also Children of Alcoholics;

Teenage alcoholism
Alcoholics Anonymous (AA), 23,
  24, 29, 45, 81, 109, 120, 121,
  33–39
  how it works, 127–28, 133–39
  meetings, 135–36
  objective of, 136
  philosophy of, 136–38
  youth attendance, 138–39
Alcoholism, meaning of, 14–15
Alcoholism and Compulsive
  Gambling Programs, 21
American College of Pathologists, 82
American Driver Traffic Safety
  Education Association, 93–94
American Indians, 33
American Medical Association, 129
Amphetamines, 29, 72–73
Amyl nitrate, 12
Anastas, Robert, 88
Angel dust, 74
Anger, 21
Anxiety, 14, 16, 39, 40, 54, 100
Asians, 34
Aspiration pneumonia, 52
Automobile Association of America
  (AAA), 84

Barbiturates, 71
Beer, 24–25, 28, 46, 47, 49, 67
Behavior patterns, 44–45

Biology, 34
Black, Claudia, 111
Blackouts, 16, 56
Blacks, 33
Blood/alcohol concentration (BAC)
    test, 81, 84–85
Blume, Dr. Sheila, 21–22, 71
Bonham, John, 52
Boy Scouts of America, 91
Brain cells, 63
Brain damage, 63–64
Brattleboro Retreat, 132
Brower, Dr. Ross, 34, 61, 66–67, 73
Butler, Charles, 84

CAGE questions, 21
Cambridge and Somerville Program
    for Alcoholism Rehabilitation
    (CASPAR), 118, 119, 139
Cancer, 58
Central nervous system, 51, 57
    brain and, 63–71
Children of alcoholics, 35–37, 99–120
    adjusters, 110–11
    experience of growing up, 99–100
    family hero, 108–9
    fear and instability, 104–5
    feelings (what to keep in mind),
        112–14
    feelings of shame, 105–8
    guilt feelings, 102–4
    mascot or family pet role, 111–12
    scapegoat, 109–10
    sources of help, 114–20
    statistics, 100–2
Chronic alcoholism, 15
Cirrhosis, 60–61, 65
Cocaine, 29, 39, 48, 49, 73
Control Factor, The, 92–93
Criminal behavior, 17–18
Cross-tolerance phenomenon, 71–72
Cultural drinking patterns, 32–34

Cutting down, 21

Daytop Village, 13, 40, 49, 130,
    131–32
    outreach program, 132–33
Delirium tremens, 14
Dependence, 66
Depression, 31, 32, 36, 40, 100, 121
Detoxification, 130
"Dial-A-Ride," 90
Digestive system, 58–62
Disease concept, 14
Downers, 71–72
Drinking, reasons and theories,
    39–50
    anxiety and depression, 39, 40
    being like an adult, 46–50
    for fun, 41–43
    genetic links, 41
    peer pressure and personality,
        43–46
    physiological problems, 40
    stimulus augmenters, 40–41
Drinking patterns, 19–20, 32–34
Drugs, 12, 20, 26, 29, 31, 39, 61, 62,
    64, 66, 69, 118
    polydrug abusers, 26, 71–74
Drunk-driving, 26, 52, 65–66, 75–98
    BAC test, 81, 84–85
    Gallup Survey (1984), 85
    Hector's and Page's experiences,
        75–82
    legal proposals, 86–87
    NHTSA statistics, 82–83
    number of teens killed each year,
        83
    programs emphasizing preven-
        tion, 87–97
Drunkenness, slang terms for, 51

Emotional immaturity, 68–69
Employee Assistance Programs, 118

INDEX

Esophagus, cancer of, 58
Ethnic stereotypes, 33
Ewing, Dr. John, 21
Explorer Post, 91
Eye-openers, 21

Family alcoholism, 35–37
Family hero role, 108–9
Family therapy, 126–27
Fatty liver, 60
Fear, feelings of, 104–5
Feelings, 40, 43, 104–8
Fetal alcohol syndrome (FAS), 65
First drink, 46
Ford, Betty, 30, 112
Ford, Steven, 112
France, 32, 33
Friendship, behavior patterns and, 45
Fun drinking, 41–43

Gallup Poll, 20, 71
Gallup Survey of Teenage Attitudes Towards and Use of Alcohol and Drugs, 85
Gastric distress, 25
Great Britain, 32
Group therapy, 125–26
Guilt, 16, 21, 23–24
    parent's drinking and, 102–4

Haggerty, David, 89–90
Hallucinations, 14
Hallucinogenic drugs, 73
Hangovers, 57
Heart and circulatory system, 62–63
Heart attacks, 62
Heavy drinkers, 18
Hepatitis, 60, 61–62
Hereditary links, 35, 41
"Hill Street Blues" (television program), 30

Holiday heart, 62
Homicides, 69
Hyperactivity, 40

Illinois Teenage Institute on Substance Abuse (ITI), 141
Independence, 68
Insurance Institute for Highway Safety, 85, 87
Intervention and family therapy, 116–18
Ireland, 32
Italy, 33

Kelly, Wells, 52

Led Zeppelin, 52
Lightner, Candy, 83
Liver damage, 15, 53, 59–62
Loss of consciousness, 25–26, 51, 59
Loss of control, 20
Loss of memory, 16, 56
Lutheran General Medical Center, 30, 131

McManus, Adam, 91
Malnutrition, 58–59
Marijuana, 12, 24, 49, 67, 73
Martin, Kiel, 30
Mascot or family pet role, 111–12
Meatloaf, 52
Menstrual irregularities, 64–65
Mescaline, 12
Minnelli, Liza, 30
Monroe, Marilyn, 72
Moore, Mary Tyler, 30
Morning drinks, 57
Mortality rate, 14, 83
Mothers Against Drunk Drivers (MADD), 83, 86
Mouth cancer, 58
Myocarditis, 62

157

National Association for Children of Alcoholics, 108

National Council on Alcoholism (NCA), 14, 16, 21, 30, 52, 60, 79, 83

National Highway Traffic Safety Administration (NHTSA), 82–83

National Institute on Alcohol Abuse and Alcoholism (NIAAA), 19, 43, 69

National Student Safety Program (NSSP), 93–94

Nausea and vomiting, 52, 73

Nelligan, Kate, 113

Operation Snowball, 141

Organ damage, 58

Outpatient treatment, 132–33

Overdoses, 52

Ozaukee Council on Alcohol and Other Drug Abuse, 140

Painkillers, 71

Pancreatitis, 58

Parkside Lodge, 30, 131

Parkside Youth Center, 131

PCP (phencyclidine), 74

Peer pressure, 43–46

Peer Resource Education Program (PREP), 139–40

Peer to peer counseling, 139–42

Personality traits, 31, 46

Physiological problems, 40

Placebo effect, 43

Polydrug abuse, 26, 71–74
    cross-tolerance, 71–72

Porter, Darrell, 30

Pregnancy, 65

Problem drinkers, 17, 26, 42
    definition of, 19
    number of, 18

Progression, 22

Progressive alcoholism, 15

Project Graduation, 88, 94–97

Pulz, Penny, 30

Reagan, Ronald, 113

Rebound effect, 57

Red Cross, 91

Religion, 34

Remove Drunk Drivers Immediately (REDD), 86

Remove Intoxicated Drivers (RID), 86

Research Triangle Institute (RTI), 19–20, 41, 43, 47, 49, 85

Residential treatment centers, 128–32

Ritchie, Kim, 87–88

Robards, Jason, 113

Rush (amyl nitrate), 12

Safe Rides system, 90–92

St. Cloud State University, 92

Sanderson, Derek, 30

Scandinavia, 32–33

Scapegoat (or "acting-out" or problem child), 109–10

Seavey, Toby, 95, 141–42

Self-esteem, 40, 108, 119

Sexual abuse, 101

Shakiness, 57

Shame, feelings of, 105–8

Shields, Brooke, 112

Shyness, 40, 67

Sleeping pills, 71

Speed, 73

Steele, Robert L., 140–41

Stillbirths, 65

Stimulus augmenters, 40–41

Student Assistance Program in Westchester County, New York, 118

INDEX

Students Against Driving Drunk
(SADD), 86, 87–90
Suicide, 69, 101

Taylor, Elizabeth, 30
Teenage alcoholism
  body and mind, 51–74
  CAGE questions, 21
  children of alcoholics, 35–37,
    99–120
  criminal behavior, 17–18
  drinking patterns, 19–20, 32–34
  drunk-driving, 26, 52, 65–66,
    75–98
  level of use, 20
  list of organizations, 145–50
  number of problem drinkers, 18
  points to keep in mind, 24–26
  problem of, 11–26
  reasons and theories of drinking,
    39–50
  See also Alcoholics
Teenage Institute for the Prevention
  of Alcohol and Other Drug
  Abuse, 141
Testicles, reduction in size of, 64
Testosterone, 64
Tolerance, 36, 54, 63
Tranquilizers, 71

Tremors, 14, 17
Twelve Steps of AA, 136–38

Ulcers, 58
United States Brewers Association,
  90
United States Department of
  Health, 52
Uppers, 72–73

Van Ost, Elaine, 117
Van Ost, Dr. William C., 110–11
Van Ost Institute for Family Living,
  110, 117
Varices, 63
Vomiting, 52, 58

Wayland Public School System
  (Wayland, Mass.), 88
Weekend drinking, 41, 42
Wegscheider, Sharon, 108
Welch, Bob, 30
West Genesee High School
  (Camillus, N.Y.), 89
Westhill High School (Stamford,
  Conn.), 91
Windham High School (Windham,
  Maine), 95
Withdrawal, 14, 17, 57, 63

ABOUT THE AUTHOR

Laurel Graeber graduated magna cum laude from Yale University and is the recipient of journalism's Atrium Award. Her writing has appeared in a number of publications, including *Seventeen, Working Woman, Travel & Leisure, Mademoiselle, House Beautiful,* and *The Christian Science Monitor.* Currently, she is a contributing editor of *Young Miss* magazine and features editor of *Daily News Record.* She lives with her husband in New York City.